SHRUBS
GEORGIA
for

SHRUBS
GEORGIA
for

Erica Glasener
Walter Reeves

COOL
SPRINGS
PRESS

Nashville, Tennessee
A Division of Thomas Nelson, Inc.
www.ThomasNelson.com

Published by Cool Springs Press, a Division of Thomas Nelson, Inc. P.O. Box 141000, Nashville, Tennessee, 37214.

First printing 2004
Printed in the United States of America
10 9 8 7 6 5 4 3 2 1

Managing Editor: Mary Morgan
Horticulture Editor: Michael Wenzel, Atlanta Botanical Garden
Copyeditor: Michelle Adkerson
Designer: Bill Kersey, Kersey Graphics
Production Artist: S.E. Anderson

On the cover: 'Hino Crimson' Azalea, photographed by Jerry Pavia

We gratefully acknowledge the contributions of the following authors who have granted their permission to use selected entries:

Pieris (pg. 76) and Purple Japanese Barberry (pg. 84)—Toby Bost; Bluebeard (pg. 16), Glossy Abelia (pg. 54), Mountain Laurel (pg. 68) and Weigela (pg. 102)—Andre Viette and Jacqueline Heriteau; Boxwood (pg. 18), Buttercup Winterhazel (pg. 26), False Cypress (pg. 46), and Flowering Quince (pg. 48)—Judy Lowe

Visit the Thomas Nelson website at www.ThomasNelson.com

Table *of* Contents

How To Use This Book

Each entry in this guide provides you with information about a plant's particular characteristics, habits, and basic requirements for active growth as well as our personal experience and knowledge of the plant. We include the information you need to help you realize each plant's potential. Only when a plant performs at its best can one appreciate it fully. You will find such pertinent information as mature height and spread, bloom period and colors, sun and soil preferences, water requirements, fertilizing needs, pruning and care, and pest information.

Sun Preferences

Symbols represent the range of sunlight suitable for each plant. Some plants can be grown in more than one range of sun, so you will sometimes see more than one sun symbol.

Full Sun   **Part Sun/Shade**   **Full Shade**

Additional Benefits

Many plants offer benefits that further enhance their appeal. The following symbols indicate some of the more important additional benefits:

 Attracts Butterflies

 Attracts Hummingbirds

 Produces Edible Fruit

 Has Fragrance

 Produces Food for Birds and Wildlife

 Drought Resistant

 Suitable for Cut Flowers or Arrangements

 Long Bloom Period

 Native Plant

 Supports Bees

 Good Fall Color

 Provides Shelter for Birds

Complementary Plants

For many of the entries, we provide landscape design ideas as well as suggestions for companion plants to help you achieve striking and personal gardening results from your garden. This is where we find the most enjoyment from gardening.

Recommended Selections

This section describes specific cultivars or varieties that are particularly noteworthy. Give them a try.

50 Great Shrubs *for* Georgia

Shrubs in Georgia come in a wide range of sizes, from ground-hugging junipers to tree-form hollies. Their flowers range from the purest white of a doublefile viburnum to the deepest blue of French hydrangea. If your taste runs to the bold statement rather than the subdued pastel, the flowers of a loropetalum or a native azalea will satisfy your needs.

Shrubs serve dual functions in a landscape. They're a solid green background for perennial and annual flowers. But many also add their own flowers and berries to the riot of color that erupts each year. The shrubs we've chosen to describe are the best of the best for Georgia. Most grow well from the seashore to the mountains. The descriptions that follow explain how to plant and grow shrubs properly, but it's also important to know how to transplant them, should you decide you'd like to move a few around, and how to prune them for good health and best effect.

Transplanting

Purple Japanese Barberry

Most shrubs should be transplanted when the demand for water is least, in late fall or winter. Since many roots inevitably will be lost, they need many weeks to regenerate themselves before the hot, dry blasts of summer arrive.

The perfect time to transplant is a cool November afternoon, a few days after a good rainfall. Small shrubs are easier to transplant than large ones, and you might need to prune away several branches to make your plant small enough to handle easily.

Plunge a shovel straight down into the soil in a circle around the plant, 12 inches from the trunk on all sides. You'll be forming a rootball 24 inches across as you proceed, each thrust of the shovel severing underground

9

roots. Just outside the slit you've made in the soil, dig an 8-inch-deep trench completely around the rootball. When you've finished the trench, place the point of the shovel at the bottom and push it beneath the rootball.

Once you've thrust beneath the shrub from all sides, get a friend to tilt the plant to one side while you slide an old shower curtain or bed sheet beneath the rootball. With a bit of huffing and puffing and root clipping, the cloth or plastic can be slid under the entire plant. Wrap it tightly around the roots to keep the soil in place.

Then carry or slide the shrub to its new home, already prepared and well dug. Plant the shrub at the same level it was growing before, and water thoroughly. When springtime comes, your shrub won't have the faintest memory of being in its old spot.

Pruning

While trees may never need pruning after they acquire their mature shape, many shrubs need regular pruning. Pruning is useful to give a shrub the proper size or shape or to help it produce more flowers.

Pruning for size may be needed simply because you want an upright oval shape between two windows rather than a wide ball that obscures your view. The best time to achieve this shaping is from February through early March. You can clip then to your heart's content, knowing the shrub will produce new leaves in a few weeks to hide any stubs or mistakes. Fast-growing shrubs such as Burford holly usually need yearly pruning to keep them inbounds.

Witchhazel

Hydrangea 'Grandiflora'

Attempt to make every pruning cut just beyond a healthy bud or small branch you'd like to preserve on the plant. One of the pleasures of pruning is doing the job with a sharp pair of by-pass (not anvil) hand pruners. When larger limbs need to be cut, a long-handled lopper makes the job a breeze. You'll achieve a much more natural shape by using hand tools rather than an electric hedge trimmer, which tempts you to fill your yard with "green meatballs."

Some shrubs produce more flowers if they're pruned severely each spring. Purple beautyberry and summersweet, for example, bear flowers in summer on branches that have grown since spring, so a light pruning in March will reward you with a thick covering of flowers. Butterfly bush needs to be cut back to 12 to 24 inches tall each March for the best flower display.

Some shrubs—azaleas, camellias, rhododendrons, and many others—produce spring blooms on branches that grew the previous year. If you prune any of these in winter, you'll remove the flower buds for the coming spring. Instead, prune them during the month after they finish flowering.

Anise
Illicium species

An Attractive Evergreen for Damp Shade

Anise is an attractive, easy-to-care-for evergreen plant that grows happily in a damp, shady spot. It is multitrunked and irregularly branched, but it forms an upright oval shape useful for screening. You can let it grow naturally or clip it. Florida anise (*Illicium floridanum*) has 1-inch, star-shaped maroon blossoms in late spring, followed by brown, waxy seed capsules. Small anise-tree (*Illicium parviflorum*) has inconspicuous yellow flowers.

Top Reasons to Plant

○ Thrives in shade
○ Evergreen foliage
○ Useful as screen or hedge
○ Attractive flowers on some types
○ Tolerates damp soil
○ Few pests or diseases

Useful Hint

When crushed, the foliage of anise smells of licorice.

Bloom Color
Maroon or yellow

Bloom Period
Late spring

Height/Width
6 to 10 feet x 5 to 10 feet

Planting Location
- Moist, well-drained soil
- Prefers morning sun and afternoon shade but tolerates more shade or more sun

Planting
- Plant in fall or spring.
- Dig the hole five times as wide as the rootball and about 12 inches deep.
- In completely boggy soil, add two or three bags of compost or soil conditioner to the soil dug from the hole.
- Place the plant in the hole and untangle the circling roots of container-grown plants.
- Refill the hole with soil and water thoroughly.
- Mulch with 2 or 3 inches of pine straw.

Watering
- The more sun the plant receives, the more water it needs.
- For fastest growth, keep the soil moist.

Fertilizing
- For the first two years after planting, feed the plant three times each year with 1 tablespoon of 10-10-10 fertilizer per foot of plant height.
- Once the plant becomes established, one feeding each spring is enough.

Easy Tip
The high shade of pine or poplar trees is perfect for anise, especially if the ground stays moist most of the time.

Suggestions for Vigorous Growth
- Prune out individual branches with hand-pruners—don't shear with hedge-trimmers.

Pest Control
- Few pests or diseases trouble this plant.
- Black vine weevils may make notches in the edges of leaves, but the damage usually isn't serious.

Complementary Plants
- Use with other shade-lovers such as nandina, winterberry, and azalea.
- Plant astilbe, ferns, and hosta underneath the anise.

Recommended Selections
- *Illicium floridanum* 'Halley's Comet' has more abundant flowers than the species.

Annabelle Hydrangea

Hydrangea arborescens 'Annabelle'

A Summer Beauty with Twelve-Inch Blooms

The blooms on 'Annabelle' are truly astounding—almost a foot wide! On close inspection, the leaves of 'Annabelle' are much softer than those of other hydrangeas, giving rise to its common name—smooth hydrangea. Winner of a Georgia Gold Medal Award, 'Annabelle' has white flowers that turn a beautiful pale-green as they age. The blooms dry so easily that it's hard to resist using them for winter arrangements.

Top Reasons to Plant

- Showy white blooms
- Good cut flower
- Good dried flower
- Blooms reliably every year
- Few pests and diseases

Useful Hint

If you plant 'Annabelle' in full sun, be sure you have a plan for regular summer irrigation.

Bloom Color
White

Bloom Period
Summer

Height/Width
4 to 6 feet x 5 to 8 feet

Planting Location
- Moist, well-drained soil with lots of organic matter
- Sun to partial shade

Planting
- Plant in spring after the last frost.
- Dig the hole five times as wide as and the same depth as the rootball.
- Mix the soil with an equal amount of compost or soil conditioner.
- Place the plant in the hole and pack soil around the roots.
- Water thoroughly.
- Mulch with pine straw or wood chips.

Watering
- Water this plant regularly—don't let 'Annabelle' dry out.
- If the leaves droop, water 'Annabelle' immediately and deeply.

Fertilizing
- During the first year, feed in March, June, and August with 1 tablespoon of 10-10-10 fertilizer per foot of plant height.
- After the first year, feed in March and June with the same amount of fertilizer.

Easy Tip

Cut off the blooms of 'Annabelle' when they begin to fade, and hang them upside down indoors to dry for winter arrangements.

Suggestions for Vigorous Growth
- 'Annabelle' produces flowers on new growth, so cut the whole plant nearly to the ground in February—the vigorous regrowth will bring blooms in late June.

Pest Control
- No serious pests or diseases trouble this plant.

Complementary Plants
- Combine 'Annabelle' with plants that draw attention away from it when it isn't flowering—Virginia sweetspire (*Itea virginica*), lantana 'Miss Huff', and purple fountain grass (*Pennisetum setaceum* 'Rubrum') are good companions in a sunny location.

Recommended Selections
- 'Grandiflora' is commonly available; its showy blooms are not as large as those of 'Annabelle'.

Bluebeard

Caryopteris × clandonensis

An Easy Shrub with Delightful Blue Flowers

Bluebeard, sometimes called blue spirea, is a small, easy, deciduous shrub that in August produces spikes of airy flowers in delightful shades of blue. The long arching branches are covered in silvery leaves, and the entire plant is delicately aromatic. It grows quickly and develops an open, airy shape that is very appealing in flower borders and makes an attractive edging along walks and paths. It blooms on new wood in midsummer or later when most other flowering shrubs are done.

Top Reasons to Plant

- Beautiful blue flowers in late summer
- Small scale
- Easy to grow
- Good cut flower
- Good dried flower
- Attracts butterflies and hummingbirds
- Few pests and diseases

Useful Hint

To improve bloom, cut bluebeard back severely—near the ground—in early spring.

Bloom Color
Shades of blue

Bloom Period
Midsummer to late summer

Height/Width
2 to 3 feet x 3 to 4 feet

Planting Location
• Well-drained, loose, loamy soil
• Sun to light shade

Planting
• Plant in early spring or early fall.
• Dig the hole five times as wide as and as deep as the rootball.
• Add compost or finely shredded bark to the planting hole and the pile of soil.
• Place the shrub in the hole and fill the hole with soil.
• Water thoroughly.
• Mulch 3 inches deep with pine straw or wood chips starting 3 inches from the crown (the place where the roots and stems meet).

Watering
• In the first year, water well every two weeks in spring and fall, and every week in summer—unless there's been an inch of rainfall per week.

Fertilizing
• Feed lightly with a slow-release, organic fertilizer in fall and again in late winter or early spring.

Easy Tip

Bluebeard foliage and flowers are both excellent in arrangements, fresh or dried.

Suggestions for Vigorous Growth
• Maintain mulch year-round.
• Since bluebeard blooms on new wood, improve flowering by pruning it back in early spring to within an inch of the living wood growth at the plant's base.

Pest Control
• No serious pests or diseases trouble this shrub.

Complementary Plants
• Plant in perennial borders for an excellent effect.
• Use in butterfly plantings.

Recommended Selections
• 'Longwood Blue' grows from $1^1/_2$ feet to 2 feet tall and has a heavy crop of deep blue flowers against silvery foliage.
• 'Dark Knight' grows to 3 feet tall by 3 to 4 feet wide with very fragrant, dark purple-blue blooms that attract butterflies and hummingbirds.
• 'Blue Mist' is about the same size as 'Dark Knight'; it has fringed blue flowers.
• 'Worcester Gold' has blue flowers and bright-yellow to chartreuse foliage.

Boxwood

Buxus species and hybrids

A Treasured Southern Evergreen for a Handsome Shrub or Hedge

Across the South, we've grown up with boxwoods. We've known them as useful foundation shrubs and as hedges. Visiting Colonial Williamsburg in Virginia and Andrew Jackson's home, the Hermitage, near Nashville, we've seen how enormous they can grow and how long they can live. Boxwoods are handsome, broadleafed evergreens with many uses; they're especially nice to add winter interest to a perennial border.

Top Reasons to Plant

○ Evergreen foliage
○ Excellent hedge plant
○ Gives winter form to perennial plantings
○ Aromatic foliage
○ Cut branches good for winter holiday decorating

Useful Hint

If planting boxwood in clay soil, amend the soil well with organic matter to improve drainage and to reduce the chance of root rot.

Height/Width
2 to 20 feet x 3 to 25 feet

Planting Location
- Moist, well-drained soil
- Sheltered from drying winds, if possible
- Sun or partial sun

Planting
- Plant in spring.
- Dig the hole five times as wide as and slightly shallower than the rootball.
- Add compost or finely shredded bark to the planting hole and the pile of soil.
- Place the shrub in the hole and fill the hole with soil.
- Water well.
- Mulch with pine straw or wood chips.

Watering
- Water deeply once a week when rainfall is lacking.

Fertilizing
- Feed each spring with a slow-release fertilizer for evergreen shrubs.

Suggestions for Vigorous Growth
- Maintain mulch year-round to protect shallow roots.
- Prune in early spring—damage may result from pruning after July.
- Use hand pruners rather than shears to avoid tearing leaves.

Easy Tip

If you want a small rounded boxwood, save yourself a lot of work—read the label and choose a cultivar that grows that way naturally.

Pest Control
- Boxwood leafminer is common—look for mottled yellow-brown leaves in August.
- Off-color foliage in spring or summer usually indicates root rot caused by poor drainage.
- Nematodes may stunt roots, particularly in coastal areas.
- If root rot or nematodes are a problem, try moving the shrub elsewhere.

Complementary Plants
- Plant in formal or colonial-style gardens.
- Use as hedges.
- Use dwarf forms to edge herb or flower gardens.

Recommended Selections
- 'Vardar Valley' is a spreading cultivar with dark blue-green foliage.
- *Buxus sempervirens* 'Elegantissima' has leaves edged in cream.

Buckeye
Aesculus parviflora

A Native Shrub with Showy Summer Flowers

What other plant has a common name that describes the two features you're sure to remember? Spectacular white bottlebrush flowers cover the bottlebrush buckeye in June. In October, the small brown nuts resembling a deer's eye fall from the branch tips. Bottlebrush buckeye is versatile—it can be a specimen shrub surrounded by pansies or a background for a perennial bed. Its fall leaf color is almost the same glowing yellow of the ginkgo tree.

Top Reasons to Plant

○ Beautiful blooms
○ Few pests or diseases
○ Thrives in shade
○ Good fall color

Useful Hint

As a woodland native, bottlebrush buckeye appreciates any attempt to approximate woodland conditions.

Bloom Color
White

Bloom Period
June

Height/Width
8 to 10 feet x 8 to 12 feet

Planting Location
• Moist, well-drained, acidic soil with organic matter added
• Prefers dappled shade but tolerates full sun to full shade

Planting
• Choose a site where it has room to grow—it spreads considerably and produces suckers, so don't crowd it.
• Plant in very early spring before growth starts.
• Dig the hole five times as wide as and the same depth as the rootball.
• Add 2 cubic feet of compost or soil conditioner to the planting hole and the pile of soil.
• Place the shrub in the hole and unwind the longest roots if they're growing densely in the container.
• Fill the hole with soil and water thoroughly.
• Mulch with pine straw or wood chips.

Watering
• For the first month, water occasionally.
• Do not let the soil dry out beneath the plant until it's well established.

Easy Tip

To pass along this gem to friends, transplant the sprouts early in spring or plant seeds immediately after they fall from the plant.

Fertilizing
• Feed with 1 tablespoon of 10-10-10 fertilizer per foot of height in April and again in midsummer.

Suggestions for Vigorous Growth
• Keep well mulched to preserve moisture.
• Dig or pull up unwanted suckers anytime of the year.

Pest Control
• No serious pests or diseases bother this plant.

Complementary Plants
• These plants make nice specimen shrubs.
• Plant beneath limbed-up tall trees or in a shrub border.

Recommended Selections
• 'Rogers' has flower clusters that are more slender but longer than those of other bottlebrush buckeyes.

Bumald Spirea

Spiraea × bumalda

A Long-Blooming Shrub with Excellent Foliage

Several species of spirea are common in Georgia landscapes, but Bumald spirea and Vanhoutte spirea (*Spiraea x vanhouttei*) are among the best. Bridal wreath spirea (*Spiraea prunifolia*) was introduced to Georgia just after the Civil War. Like most spireas, its foliage isn't very attractive after the flowers fade. Bumald spirea, though, has handsome bluish green foliage all summer, with flowers ranging from light pink to carmine.

Top Reasons to Plant

- Pretty clusters of flowers
- Long season of bloom
- Attractive foliage all summer
- Drought tolerant
- Easy to grow
- Few serious pests and diseases

Useful Hint

Bumald spirea continues producing flowers from late May through early August if you give the plant a good shearing in June.

Bloom Color
Pink to red

Bloom Period
Spring through summer

Height/Width
18 to 30 inches x 3 to 5 feet

Planting Location
- Tolerates any average soil except those that stay wet and don't drain well
- Sun

Planting
- Plant in spring in north Georgia, and spring or fall in south Georgia.
- Dig the hole three times as wide as and as deep as the rootball.
- Thoroughly break up the soil.
- Place the plant in the hole; untangle and spread out some of the larger roots.
- Fill the hole with soil.
- Water thoroughly.
- Mulch with pine straw or wood chips.

Watering
- Keep the soil evenly moist for the first four weeks after planting.
- If the plant is in sandy soil and full sun, water during summer to avoid drought stress.

Fertilizing
- Feed in March, June, and August of the first year with 1 tablespoon of 10-10-10 fertilizer per foot of plant height.
- After the first year, feed the same amount but only in March and June.

Easy Tip
Bumald spirea can be used as a ground cover; to make it spread quickly over a large area, bury the tips of the longest branches in the earth—they'll root and grow vigorously within a year.

Suggestions for Vigorous Growth
- This shrub withstands considerable drought once established, but for more flowers, water regularly.
- After the first flowers begin to fade, use hedge clippers to trim 6 inches of foliage off the entire plant to produce a second flush of blooms in July.
- Transplant sprouts that appear beneath a mature plant.

Pest Control
- Few serious pests or diseases bother this plant.

Complementary Plants
- Plant with such companion shrubs as summersweet (*Clethra alnifolia*) and fothergilla (*Fothergilla gardenii*).

Recommended Selections
- *Spiraea* x *bumalda* 'Anthony Waterer' is by far the most common cultivar.
- 'Goldflame' has brilliant orange-red leaves in spring and light-pink flowers during summer.

Burning Bush

Euonymus alatus

A Shrub That Turns Fire-Engine Red, and Then Some, in Fall

Fluorescent-red, fire-engine-red, brilliant-scarlet—attempts to describe the fall color of burning bush simply don't do it justice. This deciduous shrub is one of the most reliable plants for spectacular fall foliage. While other shrubs may look fabulous in some years, and okay in others, burning bush always comes through. Although a true star in autumn, it's modest in its requirements, being adaptable to almost any situation except wet soil and extreme drought.

Top Reasons to Plant

○ Striking fall color
○ Adaptable to varying soils
○ Few pests and diseases
○ Tolerates range of light conditions
○ Good screen or hedge plant

Useful Hint

You can remove the lower limbs of burning bush and grow it as a small tree.

Bloom Color
Insignificant yellowish flowers

Bloom Period
Late spring

Height/Width
6 to 20 feet x 10 to 20 feet

Planting Location
- Any average soil that doesn't stay wet
- Sun or partial sun for best color, but tolerates shade

Planting
- Plant in early spring.
- Dig the hole three times as wide as and slightly shallower than the rootball.
- Add compost or finely shredded bark to the planting hole and the pile of soil if the soil tends to be dry.
- Place the shrub in the hole and fill the hole with soil.
- Water thoroughly.
- Mulch with several inches of pine straw or fine pine bark.

Watering
- Regular watering is best if rainfall is below normal, but this shrub can tolerate occasional dryness.

Fertilizing
- This shrub grows slowly, so apply slow-release fertilizer in early spring each year before the plant leafs out.

Easy Tip
Burning bush has the best fall color in the cooler parts of Georgia.

Suggestions for Vigorous Growth
- Maintain mulch so the soil doesn't dry out.
- Little pruning is required, but you may shear the plant regularly if it's grown as a hedge.

Pest Control
- Few serious disease or insect problems trouble this shrub.

Complementary Plants
- Place in front of evergreens where its glowing fall color is more noticeable.
- This shrub makes a good, colorful screening plant.

Recommended Selections
- 'Compactus' isn't quite as small as its name makes it sound—about 10 feet high, though it grows slowly—but it has a nice shape and outstanding fall leaf color.
- 'Rudy Haag' is about half as tall as 'Compactus', making it great for small spaces, and its fall foliage tends to be more rosy than screaming-red.

Buttercup Winterhazel

Corylopsis pauciflora

A Dainty Charmer with Lovely, Fragrant Yellow Blooms

In spring, the bare spreading branches of the buttercup winterhazel are covered with fragrant, primrose-yellow flowers dangling in short clusters of two or three. Blooming about the same time as forsythia, it is more delicate and elegant in appearance and in size, making it an excellent choice for small yards where forsythia won't fit. Buttercup winterhazel has an attractive growing habit, pretty leaves, and straw-yellow fall foliage.

Top Reasons to Plant

- Dangling, pastel-yellow blooms
- Fragrant flowers
- Refined, graceful form
- Nice fall color
- Disease and pest resistant
- Tolerates moist soils
- Fits well into smaller gardens

Useful Hint

Buttercup winterhazel is a wonderful choice for yellow flowers in early spring in small gardens.

26

Bloom Color
Primrose-yellow

Bloom Period
Late winter to early spring

Height/Width
4 to 6 feet x 4 to 6 feet

Planting Location
• Well-drained, moist, acidic soil with lots of organic matter
• Sun to light shade

Planting
• Plant in spring.
• Dig the hole three times as wide as and slightly shallower than the rootball.
• Add compost or finely shredded bark to the planting hole and the pile of soil.
• Place the plant in the hole and fill the hole with soil.
• Water thoroughly.
• Mulch with several inches of pine straw or fine pine bark.

Watering
• Keep the soil moist while the shrub is young.
• Once the shrub becomes established, water deeply in weeks without at least an inch of rain.

Easy Tip
The only serious enemy of this easy-to-grow, elegant beauty is drought.

Fertilizing
• No fertilizer is required.
• If desired, feed the plant in early spring with a slow-release fertilizer for acid-loving shrubs.

Suggestions for Vigorous Growth
• Prune, if needed, after flowering.
• Shelter from winter winds and late frosts.

Pest Control
• No serious pests or diseases trouble this plant.

Complementary Plants
• Underplant with spring bulbs and early-flowering perennials such as blue-flowered pulmonaria.
• Mass in a woodland setting for an excellent effect.
• Plant against a dark-evergreen background.

Recommended Selections
• Plant the species.

Butterfly Bush
Buddleja davidii

A Butterfly Magnet That People Like Too

Butterfly bush is a garden mainstay with flowers all summer. The combination of scent and flower shape attracts butterflies from all over the neighborhood. The shrub occasionally seems alive from the fluttering of dozens of butterflies. For a butterfly garden, combine butterfly bush with bronze fennel (*Foeniculum vulgare*), parsley (*Petroselinum crispum*), and yarrow (*Achillea* species) to feed the caterpillars.

Top Reasons to Plant

- Beautiful plumes of flowers
- Wide range of colors
- Guaranteed to attract butterflies
- Graceful shape
- Long bloom period
- Fragrant flowers
- Few pests or diseases

Useful Hint

Place a birdbath near your butterfly plants, fill the birdbath with pebbles, and cover the pebbles with water—the butterflies will visit to bask and drink.

Bloom Color
Purple, blue, pink, yellow, or white

Bloom Period
Midsummer to frost

Height/Width
5 to 8 feet x 5 to 8 feet

Planting Location
- Best in fertile, moist, well-drained soil but tolerates just about any soil that's well drained
- Sun

Planting
- Plant in spring.
- Dig the hole three times as wide as and slightly shallower than the rootball.
- Thoroughly break up the soil.
- Place the shrub in the hole and untangle some of the larger roots, spreading them in the hole.
- Fill the hole with soil and water thoroughly.
- Mulch with several inches of pine straw or fine pine bark.

Watering
- For the first four weeks, keep the soil evenly moist.
- For the first two years, water deeply in weeks without at least an inch of rainfall.

Fertilizing
- Feed in March, June, and August with 1 tablespoon of 10-10-10 fertilizer per foot of plant height.

Easy Tip

Include nectar plants such as purple coneflower (*Echinacea purpurea*), lantana (*Lantana camara*), and common zinnia (*Zinnia elegans*) in your butterfly garden.

Suggestions for Vigorous Growth
- This plant blooms on new growth—be sure to cut the shrub back to 12 to 24 inches tall in March before leaves emerge.
- Cut off flowers as they fade.

Pest Control
- Few insects or diseases bother this shrub.
- Avoid insecticides—they'll harm the butterflies.

Complementary Plants
- Mass several together for a beautiful show.
- Use as the centerpiece of a perennial border with tall verbena (*Verbena bonariensis*), Mexican sage (*Salvia leucantha*), and Joe-pye weed (*Eupatorium maculatum*).

Recommended Selections
- 'Black Knight' has dark-purple flowers.
- 'Snowbank' has pure-white flowers.
- The Nanho varieties are more compact, growing only 3 to 5 feet high in most gardens.

Butterfly Rose

Rosa chinensis var. *mutabilis*

An Easy Beauty with Flowers of Many Colors

The butterfly rose isn't what most people think of as a classic rose. The silky, single-petaled blooms are soft-yellow when they open, but rather than fading with age as most rose blossoms do, they darken and become more intense, turning shades of orange, pink, and crimson. When this rose is in bloom and different colors flicker in the breeze, it looks as if a host of butterflies has taken up residence on the plant.

Top Reasons to Plant

- Long bloom season
- Dramatic bloom colors
- Attractive spring foliage
- Withstands cold winters
- Very disease-resistant

Useful Hint

Although it isn't evergreen, the foliage of the butterfly rose starts out bronze in spring and persists late into the fall, providing another ornamental effect we don't get from most roses.

Bloom Color
Yellow, orange, pink, and crimson

Bloom Period
Early summer until frost

Height/Width
4 to 6 feet x 3 to 4 feet

Planting Location
• Rich, well-drained soil with lots of organic matter
• Sun or partial sun

Planting
• Plant bare-root roses during their dormant season as soon as you get them.
• Plant containerized roses in early spring or early fall.
• Dig the hole 24 inches wide and as deep as the plant's roots.
• Amend the soil so it is one-third original soil, one-third coarse sand, and one-third organic matter.
• Place the plant in the hole—for bare-root roses, place the roots over a small mound of soil to allow them to spread in all directions.
• Water thoroughly.
• Fill the hole with soil, packing it firmly around the roots, and water again.
• Mulch with pine straw or wood chips.

Watering
• Water an inch each week if there hasn't been that amount of rainfall.
• Water deeply, preferably using a soaker hose, rather than sprinkling the plant often.

Easy Tip
Butterfly rose is usually grown on its own roots, rather than grafted, so if it's killed back to the ground during a severe winter, it will recover.

Fertilizing
• Apply rose fertilizer regularly using label directions.

Suggestions for Vigorous Growth
• Top-dress with mulch two or three times each year to provide additional organic matter and to help keep the roots cool and moist.
• Prune only to remove dead or diseased wood.

Pest Control
• Butterfly rose resists diseases but may be bothered by a variety of insects—consult your Extension Agent for controls for your particular needs.

Complementary Plants
• Use it in a border with annuals or perennials, but make sure you give it plenty of space to grow.

Recommended Selections
• Butterfly rose is a China rose, which is a disease-resistant, ever-blooming, long-lived class of roses—other good Chinas to try are 'Old Blush', 'Archduke Charles', and 'Ducher'.

Camellia

Camellia species

A Southern Favorite for Winter Blooms

During the camellia's blooming season, few plants can match its firepower. *Camellia sasquana* begins blooming in late fall. Many of the sasquana types are fragrant, but the blooms are smaller than those of *Camellia japonica*. It takes over in late December and may have blooms until April. Once blooming is over, the dark-green, leathery leaves of camellia make it an excellent background shrub for other flowering plants.

Top Reasons to Plant

○ Beautiful blossoms in cold weather
○ Attractive glossy, evergreen foliage
○ Usually few pests or diseases
○ Good cut flower

Useful Hint

Camellias are easy to root from cuttings, so if your neighbor has one you love, ask to take a cutting or two.

Bloom Color
Pink, white, red, yellow, blue, or variegated

Bloom Period
Fall through spring

Height/Width
6 to 8 feet x 4 to 6 feet

Planting Location
- Moist, well-drained, acidic soil amended with lots of organic matter such as fine pine bark
- Partial shade—under tall pines or on the north or east side of a structure
- Protected from wind

Planting
- Plant in fall or spring.
- Dig the hole five times as wide as the rootball and about 12 inches deep.
- Add compost or finely shredded bark to the planting hole and the pile of soil.
- Place the shrub in the hole and try to untangle any circling roots on container-grown plants.
- Fill the hole with soil and water thoroughly.
- Mulch with several inches of pine straw or fine pine bark.

Watering
- Water regularly when rainfall doesn't total an inch per week.
- This shrub's shallow root system cannot tolerate drought.

Fertilizing
- For fastest growth, feed in spring, summer, and fall with 1 tablespoon of 10-10-10 fertilizer for every foot of plant height.

Easy Tip
Although camellia flowers may be damaged by temperatures below 32 degrees Fahrenheit, unopened buds won't be harmed.

- Once camellia reaches its desired size, feed only in spring and summer using the same amount of fertilizer.

Suggestions for Vigorous Growth
- To keep the plant in shape, remove two or three leaves at the base of the bloom when you cut off faded flowers.
- Prune after flowering stops.
- To protect from severe cold snaps, cover with a blanket, mattress pad, or quilt, making sure the covering goes completely to the ground on all sides and anchoring it with stones.

Pest Control
- Swollen leaves in April denote camellia leaf gall—remove and destroy affected leaves.

Complementary Plants
- For an excellent effect, mass beneath tall pines with lower limbs 20 feet high.

Recommended Selections
- With more than twenty thousand varieties of *Camellia japonica* alone, there is a camellia for every taste.

Chinese Holly

Ilex cornuta

A Classic Evergreen with Spiny Leaves and Bright-Red Berries

Chinese hollies have various mature heights in the landscape. *Ilex cornuta* 'Rotunda' stops growing at 4 feet tall, but a mature *I. cornuta* 'Burfordii' might grow 25 feet high. All the Chinese hollies have shiny, needlelike spines on each leaf. Plants are either male or female—but only the female has berries, which make great holiday decorations. However, 'Burfordii' produces berries without pollination.

Top Reasons to Plant

○ Evergreen foliage
○ Showy red berries
○ Pest and disease resistant
○ Tolerates cold
○ Good cut greens for holiday decorations

Useful Hint

Leave plenty of room for your hollies to grow, or it will be a yearly chore to prune them—and a painful one, too, because of the spines on the leaves.

34

Bloom Color

Inconspicuous white blooms, followed by red berries in fall

Bloom Period

Spring

Height/Width

4 to 20 feet x 8 to 15 feet

Planting Location

- Well-drained, slightly acidic soil enriched with organic matter
- Sun

Planting

- Plant in fall or spring.
- Dig the hole three times as wide as and slightly shallower than the rootball.
- Place the shrub in the hole at the same depth it was growing, making sure to loosen and untangle the roots of container-grown plants that have become potbound.
- Fill the hole with soil, packing it firmly around the roots, and water well.
- Mulch with several inches of pine straw or fine pine bark.

Watering

- For the first month after planting, water holly weekly.
- Once established, Chinese holly tolerates drought and heat.

Fertilizing

- Feed in spring and again in midsummer with 1 tablespoon of 10-10-10 fertilizer per foot of plant height.

Easy Tip

Once a Chinese holly is established in the right spot, it grows for years without problems.

Suggestions for Vigorous Growth

- To keep the plant small, prune moderately in July.
- If Chinese holly needs to be drastically reduced in size, cut off everything down to a height of 12 inches in late February—the naked stump quickly sprouts new branches in spring.

Pest Control

- Scale may appear on Chinese holly.

Complementary Plants

- Depending on the type, plant as hedges and barriers.
- Use in foundation plantings.
- Use for topiaries.

Recommended Selections

- *Ilex cornuta* 'Carissa' has only a small spine on the ends of its leaves, which makes it one of the "friendlier" Chinese hollies.
- 'Burfordii' was discovered in Westview Cemetery in Atlanta; that original plant is parent to millions of Burford hollies.
- 'Rotunda' is an excellent barrier shrub—its spines make it impassable to children, adults, and pets.

Common Hydrangea

Hydrangea macrophylla

A Beloved Summer Bloomer

The common, or French, hydrangea offers many possibilities for color, foliage, and bloom time in your garden. Though the blue or pink types are most familiar, new varieties are available with deep-maroon blooms, variegated leaves, and a wide range of flower sizes and shapes. The familiar globe-shaped blooms we all recognize are often called "hortensias," but the less common lace-cap blooms, which are flatter and much daintier, are preferred by many.

Top Reasons to Plant

○ Beautiful summer blossoms
○ Excellent cut flower
○ Good dried flower
○ Thrives in partial shade
○ Few pests and diseases

Useful Hint

Many hydrangeas have blue blooms in acidic soils and pink ones in alkaline soils—adding lime to the soil may make the blue types turn pink, while adding sulfur does the opposite.

Bloom Color
Pink, blue, red, or white

Bloom Period
Summer

Height/Width
2 to 6 feet x 2 to 8 feet

Planting Location
- Moist, well-drained soil with lots of organic matter
- Partial shade (morning sun and afternoon shade)
- Within reach of the hose

Planting
- Plant in fall in south Georgia and after April 15 from Atlanta northward.
- Dig the hole five times as wide as and slightly shallower than the rootball.
- Add enough compost or finely shredded bark to the planting hole and the pile of soil so that the soil is half original and half organic matter.
- Place the shrub in the hole and firm the soil around the roots.
- Water thoroughly.
- Mulch with several inches of pine straw or fine pine bark.

Watering
- Regular watering is essential.
- In hot summer months, you may need to water twice a week if rainfall isn't adequate.
- Watch for signs of wilting—that tells you to water!

Fertilizing
- In the first year, feed in March, June, and August with 1 tablespoon of 10-10-10 fertilizer per foot of height.

Easy Tip
Keep in mind that hydrangea's love for water is right there in its name—"hydro," the Latin word for water.

- After the first year, feed in March and June using the same amount of fertilizer.

Suggestions for Vigorous Growth
- If needed, prune in late June, immediately after the flowers fade.
- Rejuvenate any hydrangea by cutting it back to a foot tall.
- Remove flower heads just after they've faded, then use them indoors in dried arrangements.

Pest Control
- No serious pests or diseases trouble this plant.

Complementary Plants
- Use in combination with camellias, rhododendrons, and azaleas.
- Hydrangeas also provide a nice backdrop for astilbe and bleeding heart.

Recommended Selections
- 'Nikko Blue' is a standard with deep-blue flowers.
- 'Ami Pasquier' produces pink blooms even in acidic soil.
- 'Lanarth White' has white, lace-cap blooms.
- 'Pia' is a pink dwarf hydrangea.

Crapemyrtle
Lagerstroemia indica

A Spectacular Summer Bloomer in Many Sizes and Colors

A crapemyrtle has three elements of beauty: its flowers, its bark, and its fall foliage color. Flower color ranges from pure-white ('Natchez') to medium-purple ('Powhatan'), with lots of reds and pinks in between. Several crapemyrtles have bark that peels off to reveal a cinnamon or gray underbark in winter. Fall leaf color, ranging from bright-yellow to deep-red, is outstanding in every corner of Georgia.

Top Reasons to Plant

- Beautiful summer blooms
- Outstanding fall foliage
- Gorgeous winter bark
- Pest and disease resistant
- Wide range of colors
- Sizes ranging from tiny to huge
- Good cut flower

Useful Hint

Avoid purchasing plants labeled only "White Crapemyrtle" or "Pink Crapemyrtle"—they'll definitely be lower quality plants and probably susceptible to powdery mildew.

Bloom Color
Red, white, pink, lavender, or purple

Bloom Period
Summer

Height/Width
3 to 20 feet x 3 to 15 feet

Planting Location
- Moist, well-drained soil
- Sun

Planting
- Plant in spring or fall.
- Dig the hole three times as wide as and the same depth as the rootball.
- Thoroughly break up the soil.
- Place the shrub in the hole and fill the hole with soil.
- Water thoroughly.
- Mulch with several inches of pine straw or fine pine bark.

Watering
- For the first year, water deeply when less than an inch of rain has fallen during the week.

Fertilizing
- Feed in April of each year with 1 tablespoon of 10-10-10 fertilizer per foot of plant height.

Suggestions for Vigorous Growth
- To increase the blooming time, remove spent blooms.
- Remove the small sprouts from the trunks of multitrunked crapemyrtles each winter.

Easy Tip

Keep crapemyrtle mulched year-round to prevent errant lawnmowers and weed-trimmers from bumping the shrub's thin bark.

Pest Control
- Aphids love to suck sap from crapemyrtle leaves; these pests secrete a sticky "honeydew" that may turn black due to sooty mold—check with your Extension Agent for controls.

Complementary Plants
- Crapemyrtles are fine specimen plants, especially near a walkway so the bark can be seen up close.

Recommended Selections
- The National Arboretum has released several outstanding disease-resistant crapemyrtles—'Natchez', 'Muskogee', 'Lipan', 'Tonto', 'Yuma', and 'Sioux' are among the best.

Doublefile Viburnum

Viburnum plicatum

A Terrific Spring Performer with a Unique Look

The flowers on a doublefile viburnum are unlike those on any other shrub. The limbs on this viburnum grow in horizontal layers up the trunk, each tier higher and smaller than the last, resulting in an effect like a tall, layered green cake. When the flowers come in April, they emerge on the top of each branch, covering it all the way to the tip. The green cake appears to have white icing—a spectacular sight!

Top Reasons to Plant

○ Beautiful spring blooms
○ Unusual horizontal branching structure
○ Red berries in late summer
○ Burgundy foliage in fall
○ Attracts birds
○ Blooms well in partial shade
○ Few pests or diseases

Useful Hint

Plant doublefile viburnum where it has room to grow and show off—do not interfere with the natural, elegant shape of this wide-spreading shrub.

Bloom Color
White

Bloom Period
Mid-spring

Height/Width
8 to 10 feet x 8 to 10 feet

Planting Location
- Moist, well-drained, slightly acidic soil with lots of organic matter
- Sun to partial shade

Planting
- Plant in spring in north Georgia and fall in south Georgia.
- Dig the hole five times as wide as and slightly shallower than the rootball.
- Add compost or finely shredded bark to the planting hole and the pile of soil.
- Place the shrub in the hole and spread the roots in the hole.
- Fill the hole with soil, making sure the plant is at the same depth as it grew before.
- Water thoroughly.
- Mulch with several inches of pine straw or fine pine bark.

Watering
- Water regularly for the first three weeks, then be alert for signs of wilting. If needed, water well.
- Once the shrub becomes established, water deeply during summer dry spells.

Fertilizing
- During the first year, feed in March, June, and August with 1 tablespoon of 10-10-10 fertilizer per foot of plant height.

Easy Tip
Watch your viburnum in late July for red berries—you'll have to keep an eye out for them because birds find them delicious.

- After the first year, feed in April and June using the same amount of fertilizer.

Suggestions for Vigorous Growth
- Keep mulched year-round.
- No pruning is needed—or desirable—except to remove broken branches.

Pest Control
- Watch for Japanese beetles, and consult your Extension Agent for controls if they appear—do *not* use beetle traps; they just attract more beetles.

Complementary Plants
- Use as a specimen plant or as a focal point in a perennial border.
- Group several for informal hedging or screening.

Recommended Selections
- With its large flowers and graceful, layered branches, 'Shasta' is by far the best doublefile viburnum.
- 'Mariesii' is also outstanding, with limbs that are so strongly horizontal the shrub in bloom looks like a table covered with a white tablecloth.

Dwarf Fothergilla

Fothergilla gardenii

A Southeastern Native That Shines in Two Seasons

The flowers of fothergilla are distinctive (they look like white bottlebrushes), but its most memorable characteristic may be its fall leaf color. A group of three or five shrubs in a corner of your landscape can make a dazzling yellow, red, and orange kaleidoscope in October. *Fothergilla major* grows to 10 feet tall, probably too large for a suburban landscape. Because dwarf fothergilla (*F. gardenii*) remains small, it can be an attractive addition to a perennial border.

Top Reasons to Plant

- Showy spring flowers
- Fragrant blossoms
- Outstanding fall foliage
- Few pests and diseases
- Easy care
- Excellent in naturalized settings

Useful Hint

Fothergilla is an arresting sight twice a year—spring flowering and fall color—but its green foliage isn't very interesting during summer.

Bloom Color
White

Bloom Period
April and May

Height/Width
3 feet x 3 feet

Planting Location
- Moist, acidic, well-drained soil
- Under high pine trees or in a slightly shady spot on the west side of the lawn

Planting
- Plant in fall or spring.
- Dig the hole three times as wide as and the same depth as the rootball.
- Pulverize the soil before packing it around the roots.
- Place the shrub in the hole and fill the hole with soil.
- Mulch with several inches of pine straw or fine pine bark.

Watering
- This shrub requires regular moisture all its life.
- Water deeply whenever the plant appears parched.

Fertilizing
- Feed in April, June, and August each year with 1 tablespoon of 10-10-10 fertilizer per foot of plant height.

Easy Tip
Summer drought or too much sun can cause the fall foliage of fothergilla to be less than fiery.

Suggestions for Vigorous Growth
- Maintain mulch year-round.
- Dwarf fothergilla tends to sucker—dig up and transplant the suckers if you don't want your plant to grow wider.
- Pruning is rarely needed.

Pest Control
- Few insects or diseases bother this shrub.

Complementary Plants
- Plant blue aster (*Aster novae-angliae*) in front of dwarf fothergilla and a blue baptisia (*Baptisia australis*) on each side for a good color contrast.
- Combine dwarf fothergilla with azalea, which likes the same type of soil.

Recommended Selections
- The very hardy *Fothergilla gardenii* 'Mt. Airy', selected by Dr. Michael Dirr of the University of Georgia, features blue-green summer leaves and spectacular yellow-orange-red fall foliage.

Fairy Rose

Rosa 'The Fairy'

A Tough, Long-Blooming Polyantha Rose

'The Fairy' is especially good in containers or at the front of a flower border. Although small, the clusters of slightly fragrant flowers put on a good show throughout the summer and into the fall, standing out against the tiny, glossy, light-green foliage. The sprays of blooms hold up well as cut flowers. Unlike many short-lived miniature roses that can be magnets for pests and diseases, 'The Fairy' is a tough survivor that has persisted in Georgia gardens for years.

Top Reasons to Plant

- ○ Jewel-like blossoms
- ○ Fragrant blooms
- ○ Fits into small spaces
- ○ Tolerates cold
- ○ Does well in containers
- ○ Good cut flower

Useful Hint

'The Fairy' is sometimes sold as a standard—a plant grown and pruned to resemble a small tree.

44

Bloom Color
Pink

Bloom Period
Summer to fall

Height/Width
3 to 4 feet x 2 to 4 feet

Planting Location
- Well-drained, fertile, moist soil with lots of organic matter
- Sun to partial shade

Planting
- Plant bare-root roses during their dormant season as soon as you get them.
- Plant containerized roses in early spring or early fall.
- Dig the hole 24 inches wide and as deep as the plant's roots.
- Amend the soil so it is one-third original soil, one-third coarse sand, and one-third organic matter.
- Place the plant in the hole—for bare-root roses, place the roots over a small mound of soil to allow them to spread in all directions.
- Water thoroughly.
- Fill the hole with soil, packing it firmly around the roots, and water again.
- Mulch with pine straw or wood chips.

Watering
- Provide an inch of water each week if there hasn't been that amount of rainfall.
- Water deeply, preferably using a soaker hose.

Easy Tip

The Fairy' is best suited for the front of a flowerbed or a container where its flowers can be viewed up close.

Fertilizing
- Apply rose fertilizer regularly using label directions.

Suggestions for Vigorous Growth
- Top-dress with mulch two or three times each year to provide additional organic matter and to help keep roots cool and moist.
- Prune in early spring when the buds begin swelling.
- Cut back plants to about 1 to 2 feet to encourage new growth and blooms.

Pest Control
- 'The Fairy' resists diseases but may be bothered by a variety of insects—consult your Extension Agent for controls for your particular problems.

Complementary Plants
- Mass together for the best effect—individual plants are too small to be effective alone.
- Plant as a border for a perennial or shrub bed.

Recommended Selections
- Some miniature roses to try are 'Perle d'Or', 'La Marne', and 'Marie Pavie'.

False Cypress

Chamaecyparis species and hybrids

Excellent Needled Evergreens with Interesting Shapes

Why grow a shrub whose name you can't pronounce? Well, it increases your choice of needled evergreens. Then there's the interesting appearance—upright or drooping, dwarf or 50 feet tall, needles of green or gold. The main useful species are Hinoki false cypress (*Chamaecyparis obtusa*) and Sawara false cypress (*Chamaecyparis pisifera*). Just be sure to read the plant's label to understand its eventual size. Oh yes, just say Kam-uh-SIP-a-ris.

Top Reasons to Plant

- Evergreen needled foliage
- Yellow or green needles
- Variety of shapes and sizes
- Few pests and diseases
- Striking specimen
- Many different uses, depending on type

Useful Hint

Match the type of *Chamaecyparis* to the spot where you need an evergreen shrub—short or tall? Upright or weeping? Green or gold?

Height/Width

4 to 20 feet x 6 to 8 feet

Planting Location

- Moist, well-drained soil enriched with organic matter
- Sun

Planting

- Plant in spring or early autumn.
- Dig the hole three times as wide as and slightly shallower than the rootball.
- Add compost or finely shredded bark to the planting hole and the pile of soil.
- Place the shrub in the hole and fill the hole with soil.
- Water thoroughly.
- Mulch with several inches of pine straw or fine pine bark.

Watering

- Water when there hasn't been an inch of rainfall during the week, especially during hot weather.
- Soak the soil thoroughly when watering.

Fertilizing

- Feed with a fertilizer for evergreens at the end of November or with a slow-release shrub fertilizer at the end of March.

Suggestions for Vigorous Growth

- Shape regularly—it's difficult to prune an overgrown evergreen without causing bare branches.

Easy Tip

The weeping forms of false cypress look wonderful cascading down a slope or over a wall.

- In late winter, remove dead stems and needles from the shrub's interior.
- Pinch tips of branches in late spring or early summer.

Pest Control

- Few insects and diseases trouble this shrub.

Complementary Plants

- Dwarfs look good in rock gardens.
- Many work well in foundation plantings or shrub borders.
- Unusual forms make excellent specimen shrubs.

Recommended Selections

- *Chamaecyparis pisifera* 'Golden Mop' is a dwarf with a threadleaf form (corded branches) that can only be described as "cute."
- *Chamaecyparis obtusa* 'Nana' remains 2 to 3 feet tall and wide; it's a nice choice in rock gardens.

Flowering Quince

Chaenomeles species and hybrids

An Old-Fashioned, Almost Indestructible Bloomer for Earliest Spring

The earlier a plant blooms in spring, the more welcome it is. That's why flowering quince has been planted across the South for generations. For many, the fact that the bright-red flowers don't last longer than a week or two doesn't matter a bit. This is a plant that welcomes spring, promising that warm weather and glorious summer are on their way.

Top Reasons to Plant

○ Vibrant early-spring blooms
○ Long lived
○ Few pests and diseases
○ Good cut flower
○ Branches force well indoors
○ Tolerates drought once established
○ Almost indestructible

Useful Hint

Plant flowering quince where it can show off in spring but recedes into the background in summer—after it blooms, it turns into a plain Jane.

Bloom Color
Red, pink, white, or orange

Bloom Period
Early spring

Height/Width
2 to 10 feet x 3 to 10 feet

Planting Location
•Well-drained, acidic soil with organic matter added to poor soil
•Sun

Planting
•Plant in spring.
•Dig the hole three times as wide as and slightly shallower than the rootball.
•Thoroughly break up the soil.
•Place the shrub in the hole and fill the hole with soil.
•Water thoroughly.
•Mulch with several inches of pine straw or fine pine bark.

Watering
•When the plant is young, water to keep the soil moist.

Fertilizing
•In early years, feed in early spring with a shrub fertilizer.

Suggestions for Vigorous Growth
•Unless pruning for use indoors, wait to prune till after all blooming has finished.
•Renew an overgrown shrub by cutting one-third of the stems back to the ground each year for three years.

Easy Tip

Cut branches in full bloom for indoor vases, or cut branches just beginning to bud for indoor forcing in late winter.

Pest Control
•If aphids appear, wash them off with a blast of water and spray with insecticidal soap.
•If many leaves drop in summer, it's usually due to excess rainfall and humidity.

Complementary Plants
•Use for a deciduous barrier hedge due to its thorns.
•Combine with early-spring-flowering bulbs in compatible colors.

Recommended Selections
•'Cameo' grows to 4 to 5 feet, with double, apricot-pink blooms and no thorns.
•'Texas Scarlet' has abundant red blooms on a spreading plant no more than 3 to 3$^1/_2$ feet high.
•'Spitfire', an upright rather than spreading form, has vivid red flowers.

Forsythia

Forsythia × intermedia

A Glorious Yellow Spring Show-Off with Graceful Habits

A familiar harbinger of spring, this yellow-flowered, deciduous shrub quickly grows to a large plant. Its slender stems arch constantly outward, so forsythia is always wider than it is tall. Left unpruned, it becomes a very graceful shrub with bell-shaped flowers appearing before the leaves, usually in early February. Though forsythia fades into the landscape for most of the year, its yellow flowers are our first true sign that spring is on the way.

Top Reasons to Plant

- Beautiful yellow blooms in early spring
- Graceful form
- Good cut flower
- Excellent for forcing in winter
- Resistant to pests and diseases
- Tolerates variety of soils
- Comes in wide range of sizes

Useful Hint

When the buds begin to swell in January, cut branches 18 to 24 inches long, bring them indoors to a warm room, and place them in a vase of water—the buds begin opening almost overnight.

Bloom Color
Yellow

Bloom Period
Early spring

Height/Width
4 to 8 feet x 6 to 10 feet

Planting Location
- Moist, well-drained soil with organic matter is best but tolerates any average soil
- Sun to mostly sun

Planting
- Plant in fall.
- Dig the hole three times as wide as and slightly shallower than the rootball.
- Thoroughly break up the soil so it has no clumps.
- Place the shrub in the hole and unwind any roots that have circled the container.
- Fill the hole with soil and water thoroughly.
- Mulch with several inches of pine straw or fine pine bark.

Watering
- For the first month, water to keep the soil moist.
- Once the shrub becomes established, watering is rarely needed.

Fertilizing
- Feed with 1 tablespoon of 10-10-10 fertilizer per foot of plant height in spring and again in midsummer.

Easy Tip
Never prune forsythia into a round ball or cut off its top—prune it correctly, and you'll retain its beautiful, natural weeping habit.

Suggestions for Vigorous Growth
- Each year, remove the oldest branches from the bush since most of the flowers emerge on two- to three-year-old branches.
- To rejuvenate an overgrown shrub, after flowering is finished, cut one-third of the stems back to ground level each year for three years.

Pest Control
- Few pests and diseases trouble this plant.

Complementary Plants
- Plant large-cupped, gold-flowered daffodils nearby for a color echo.
- Position in a group of other plants with flowers at other times of the year.

Recommended Selections
- 'Lynwood Gold' is a widely available cultivar.
- 'Arnold's Dwarf' doesn't flower heavily but can be a useful ground cover.
- 'Karl Sax' has very large, deep-yellow flowers.

Gardenia

Gardenia jasminoides

A Fragrant Beauty That Is the Essence of Summer

For some Georgians, the smell of gardenia flowers on a warm June afternoon is the emblem of summer. Though the glossy green foliage is handsome, the flowers and their scent are what most people love about this shrub. Only marginally hardy north of Atlanta, from mid-Georgia southward, gardenia is a reliable specimen shrub or component of a shrub border. Several gardenias together can perfume a whole neighborhood.

Top Reasons to Plant

- Beautiful creamy-white blooms
- Fragrant flowers
- Glossy evergreen foliage
- Good cut flower

Useful Hint

Gardenias can be finicky—give them acidic soil, good drainage, and regular water and fertilizer.

52

Bloom Color
- White

Bloom Period
Spring into fall, depending on cultivar

Height/Width
4 to 6 feet x 4 to 6 feet

Planting Location
- Moist, well-drained, acidic soil with lots of organic matter
- Sun to partial shade
- Protected from winter winds and winter sun

Planting
- Plant in spring.
- Dig the hole three times as wide as and slightly more shallow than the rootball.
- Thoroughly break up the soil.
- Place the plant in the hole and unwind any roots that have circled the container.
- Pack soil around the roots and water thoroughly.
- Mulch with pine straw to conserve moisture.

Watering
- Water occasionally for the first month.
- Water deeply during periods of drought or high temperatures.

Fertilizing
- Feed in spring and again in midsummer with 1 tablespoon of 10-10-10 fertilizer per foot of plant height.

Easy Tip

An eastern or northern exposure is a better choice for gardenia than a south-facing wall, where it will almost certainly freeze to the ground each winter.

Suggestions for Vigorous Growth
- If extreme cold threatens, cover the gardenia with an old bed sheet, making sure it goes down to the ground on all sides and anchoring it with stones or heavy limbs.
- In shade, lower limbs may fall off, leaving a bare trunk—prune the whole shrub back to 12 inches tall in late March, and let it resprout.

Pest Control
- Whiteflies are common gardenia pests—check with your Extension Agent for an effective insecticide.

Complementary Plants
- Plant as part of a shrub border.

Recommended Selections
- 'Kleim's Hardy' resists cold.
- 'Michael' resists both cold and whiteflies.

Glossy Abelia

Abelia × grandiflora

An Easy-Goer with a Summer-Long Flower Show

Glossy abelia's great asset is a summer-long show of flowers—it comes into bloom in April or May and continues until frost. This rounded, multistemmed, semievergreen shrub has dainty foliage and small, slightly fragrant, funnel-shaped pink flowers beloved by pollinating insects. The leaves take on a purplish bronze cast in late fall and last until early winter in the coldest parts of Georgia, hanging on all winter in warmer regions.

Top Reasons to Plant

- Long season of bloom
- Fragrant flowers
- Dainty, semievergreen foliage
- Purplish fall color
- Pest and disease resistant
- Attracts butterflies

Useful Hint

Abelia 'Sunrise' has gold leaf margins, and 'Confetti' is a white variation—both are stunning planted with crapemyrtles and coarse-textured evergreens.

Bloom Color
Pink

Bloom Period
May or June until frost

Height/Width
3 to 6 feet x 5 feet

Planting Location
• Well-drained, acidic soil with lots of organic matter
• Sun to partial sun

Planting
• Plant in early spring or early fall.
• Dig the hole three times as wide as and slightly shallower than the rootball.
• Thoroughly break up the soil so no clumps remain.
• Place the shrub in the hole and fill the hole with soil.
• Water thoroughly.
• Mulch with several inches of pine straw or fine pine bark.

Watering
• During the plant's first year, water well every two weeks in spring and fall, and every seven to ten days in summer, unless there's been an inch of rainfall during the week.

Fertilizing
• Feed lightly in fall and early spring with a slow-release fertilizer for acid-loving plants.

Easy Tip
Abelia is a great plant for foraging honeybees and it never needs spraying.

Suggestions for Vigorous Growth
• In late winter, prune back dead branch tips to outward-facing buds.
• Prune off winterkilled tips in early spring.
• Once the shrub reaches a pleasing size, maintain it by removing up to a third of the branch tips each year after flowering is over.
• Maintain mulch year-round.

Pest Control
• Few pests and diseases bother this plant.

Complementary Plants
• Use to cover a bank for an excellent effect.

Recommended Selections
• 'Edward Goucher' is a tried-and-true favorite, growing 3 to 6 feet tall, with dense, arching growth and lilac-pink flowers. It makes a good informal hedge or specimen.
• 'Prostrata', a low-growing, compact shrub, has smaller leaves that turn burgundy-green in winter.

Japanese Holly

Ilex crenata

An Excellent Evergreen Shrub with Many Uses

Japanese hollies have small leaves, generally 1-inch long and ¹/₂-inch wide, and are usually pruned regularly to form a 3- to 5-foot foundation shrub or hedge. Japanese hollies are the underappreciated green backbone of thousands of homes and commercial landscapes. Two types—'Convexa' and 'Buxifolia'—look like boxwoods and are good substitutes for them.

Top Reasons to Plant

○ Evergreen foliage
○ Few pests and diseases
○ Tolerates variety of soils
○ Accepts pruning
○ Easy to grow

Useful Hint

Break up the monotony of a solid line of Japanese hollies by including a small camellia or azalea in a similar size.

Bloom Color
No significant blooms

Bloom Period
Foliage effective year-round

Height/Width
2 to 10 feet x 2 to 8 feet

Planting Location
- Well-drained, slightly acidic soil
- Sun to partial shade

Planting
- Plant in fall or spring.
- Dig the hole three times as wide as and the same depth as the rootball.
- Thoroughly break up the soil, leaving no clumps.
- Place the plant in the hole and untangle the roots if they've grown in a circle around the container.
- Pack soil around the roots, making sure the plant is at the same depth it was growing.
- Water thoroughly.
- Mulch with pine straw or wood chips.

Watering
- Keep plants watered until they are established and growing.
- Hollies growing under the roof overhang will need water during times of drought.

Fertilizing
- Feed in spring and again in midsummer with 1 tablespoon of 10-10-10 fertilizer per foot of plant height.

Easy Tip
Electric hedge trimmers are "Public Enemy Number One" of Japanese hollies—pruning by hand results in a healthier, more attractive shrub.

Suggestions for Vigorous Growth
- Prune by hand, not with electric hedge trimmers—with just a few years of regular shearing, a dense outer shell of greenery will grow around an interior of naked brown twigs.
- Remove long branches regularly in summer—any hole left will be filled in quickly by branches on either side.

Pest Control
- No serious pests or diseases bother this plant.

Complementary Plants
- Use as an evergreen backdrop for colorful flowers and shrubs.

Recommended Selections
- 'Helleri' grows from 1 to 3 feet tall.
- 'Hetzii' is taller, growing to 3 to 5 feet, and is adaptable to just about any site.
- 'Green Luster' grows much wider than tall.
- 'Beehive' has good-looking foliage and is very hardy.

Juniper

Juniperus species and hybrids

The Rodney Dangerfield of Shrubs

Junipers are shrubs that get no respect. They are as common as dirt, tough as nails, and green year-round. If a broadleafed shrub performed this well, it would be hailed throughout the country, yet junipers are not honored at all. We rarely appreciate the terrific durability and variability of this everyday shrub. While they may be common, junipers get the landscape job done without complaint.

Top Reasons to Plant

○ Evergreen foliage effective year-round
○ Wide range of sizes and uses
○ Durable and reliable
○ Drought tolerant
○ Needs little care
○ Adapts to wide variety of soils

Useful Hint

Juniper has many cultivars—read the plant information tag carefully to make sure the one you have selected is the size and shape you want.

Height/Width
6 to 12 feet x 3 to 15 feet

Planting Location
- Any soil as long as it isn't soggy—improve drainage by adding organic matter
- Full sun

Planting
- Plant in early spring in north Georgia and in spring or fall in south Georgia.
- Dig the hole twice as wide as and slightly shallower than the rootball.
- Thoroughly break up the soil, leaving no clods.
- Place the shrub in the hole and fill the hole with soil.
- Water thoroughly.
- Mulch with several inches of pine straw or fine pine bark.

Watering
- Water regularly for the first year or two.
- Thereafter, junipers tolerate drought.

Fertilizing
- For the first two years, feed in spring, midsummer, and fall with 1 tablespoon of 10-10-10 fertilizer per foot of plant height or spread.
- From the third year onward, feed each spring with ¼ cup of 10-10-10 per foot of plant height or spread.

Suggestions for Vigorous Growth
- Keep mulched year-round—the decomposing mulch provides gentle feeding.
- Promptly prune off damaged branches.
- Prune as needed in early spring to shape and control size.

Easy Tip
Once established, junipers are among the most durable and versatile of plants.

Pest Control
- Mites may appear—use a water spray to dislodge them or ask your Extension Agent about chemical controls.
- Bagworms may be a problem on stressed plants—pick them off in August.
- If tips die back in spring on young junipers, a disease called *Phomopsis* may be present—control the disease by removing and disposing of affected shoots.

Complementary Plants
- Taller types make excellent hedges and screens and good evergreen backdrops for showy, blooming shrubs and flowers.
- Low-growing types are excellent ground covers and slope-holders.

Recommended Selections
- *Juniperus chinensis* 'Blue Point' is an easy-to-find upright variety.
- *Juniperus horizontalis* 'Blue Rug' and 'Bar Harbor' are two good low-growing, spreading junipers.

Lady Banks' Rose

Rosa banksiae 'Alba-Plena', *Rosa banksiae* 'Lutea'

An Outstanding Easy-Care Climber

Lady Banks', a vigorous climber, is outstanding among the roses that thrive in Georgia with little or no care. One of the first roses to bloom in spring, its scent has been compared to violets. When in bloom, it looks like a blanket of flowers covers the plant for up to six weeks. These long-lived and vigorous plants may threaten to pull down buildings when the trunks get as big around as small trees.

Top Reasons to Plant

○ Beautiful blossoms
○ Long bloom season
○ Fragrant flowers on white variety
○ No serious pests or diseases
○ Grows rapidly
○ Attractive foliage year-round

Useful Hint

Be patient after planting Lady Banks' rose—it will be a few years before you see good blooms.

Bloom Color
Yellow or white

Bloom Period
Spring

Height/Width
15 to 20 feet x 8 to 12 feet

Planting Location
- Moist, well-drained, fertile soil
- Sun to partial shade

Planting
- Plant bare-root roses during their dormant season as soon as you get them.
- Plant containerized roses in early spring or early fall.
- Dig the hole 24 inches wide and as deep as the plant's roots.
- Amend the soil so it is one-third original soil, one-third coarse sand, and one-third organic matter.
- Place the plant in the hole—for bare-root roses, place the roots over a small mound of soil to allow them to spread in all directions.
- Water thoroughly.
- Fill the hole with soil, packing it firmly around the roots, and water again.
- Mulch with pine straw or wood chips.

Watering
- Provide an inch of water each week if there hasn't been that amount of rainfall.
- Water deeply, preferably using a soaker hose.

Fertilizing
- Apply rose fertilizer regularly using label directions.

Easy Tip
The willowlike foliage of the Lady Banks' rose looks good year-round.

Suggestions for Vigorous Growth
- Top-dress with mulch two or three times each year to provide additional organic matter and to help keep roots cool and moist.
- Prune every other year—Lady Banks' flowers on second- and third-year wood, so prune carefully, removing only old, less vigorous wood.
- Tie in the long shoots to whatever support you're using for Lady Banks'.

Pest Control
- No serious pests or diseases trouble this plant.

Complementary Plants
- Train Lady Banks' up a tree or over a high wall where the foliage can cascade down.

Recommended Selections
- The yellow Lady Banks' rose (*R. banksiae* 'Lutea') is unscented but is slightly hardier than the white form (*R. banksiae* 'Alba-Plena').

Lilac

Syringa species

A Northern Favorite for Georgia Gardens

One of the first plants transplanted Northerners miss in the South is the lilac. They wonder why such a glorious plant is neglected here. The answer is simple: Lilacs need hundreds of hours of cold weather to bloom, and except for the Georgia mountains, those hours aren't available here. Fortunately, a few types do bloom with little cold and have a chance of flourishing in middle Georgia.

Top Reasons to Plant

○ Lavish blooms
○ Fragrant flowers

Useful Hint

If you plant a lilac needing lots of winter chill, you'll likely get nothing but leaves, and they'll have powdery mildew—choose one of the recommended selections for planting in Georgia.

Bloom Color
Lavender, blue, or pink

Bloom Period
Mid- to late spring

Height/Width
6 to 10 feet x 5 to 8 feet

Planting Location
- Moist, fertile, well-drained soil
- Open area with good air circulation
- Full sun

Planting
- Plant in spring.
- Space plants at least 5 to 8 feet apart to prevent overcrowding.
- Dig the hole three times as wide as and slightly shallower than the rootball.
- Add one bag of soil conditioner to form a low mound on which to plant.
- Place the shrub in the hole and untangle the roots, spreading them in the hole. Fill the hole with soil and water thoroughly.
- Mulch with several inches of pine straw or fine pine bark.

Watering
- Keep the plant moist until it becomes established.
- Water deeply using a soaker hose in weeks without an inch of rainfall.

Fertilizing
- No fertilizer is required, but for faster growth, feed with 1 tablespoon of 10-10-10 fertilizer per foot of plant height in April and June.
- When the plant reaches the size you desire, fertilize it only in April with the same amount as before.

Easy Tip

Many Southern gardeners find that Persian lilac (*Syringa × persica*) performs better than the common lilac (*Syringa vulgaris*), though it, too, is subject to powdery mildew.

Suggestions for Vigorous Growth
- After flowering, prune back to the first two side branches below the spot where the flowers grew.
- Once the lilac is large, remove a couple of older stems each year.

Pest Control
- Powdery mildew affects most lilacs, disfiguring the plants, unless you have a resistant variety.

Complementary Plants
- Use for shrub borders or mass plantings.

Recommended Selections
- *Syringa vulgaris* 'President Lincoln' and *Syringa patula* 'Miss Kim' have done well at Barnsley Gardens in Adairsville.
- *Syringa vulgaris* 'Blue Boy' and 'Lavender Lady' were developed in California for mild winter environments.
- The cut-leaf lilac (*S. laciniata*) blooms reliably each year, though its blooms aren't as large as the Northern lilacs.

Loropetalum

Loropetalum chinense var. *rubrum*

A Showy Evergreen with Burgundy Leaves

The new loropetalums have purple leaves and bright (screamingly bright!) fuchsia blooms. This member of the witchhazel family grows rapidly, has showy foliage year-round, blooms heavily in spring, and is generally carefree and pest free. It is usually hardy from Atlanta southward, but a severe winter in the northern third of Georgia will freeze many loropetalums to the ground. Fortunately, they quickly regrow the following year.

Top Reasons to Plant

○ Burgundy to red foliage year-round
○ Bright fuzzy blooms in spring
○ Graceful, arching form
○ Easy to force indoors
○ Fragrant flowers
○ Adaptable to varying light conditions

Useful Hint

Loropetalum is a graceful spreader that grows quite tall, so site it where you don't have to butcher its shape by pruning.

Bloom Color
Pink or white

Bloom Period
Spring (and sometimes later)

Height/Width
2 to 6 feet x 2 to 8 feet

Planting Location
- Prefers moist, well-drained, acidic soil—but tolerates clay or sand
- Sun or partial shade

Planting
- Plant in spring in the northern half of the state and spring or fall in the southern half.
- Dig the hole three times as wide as and slightly shallower than the rootball.
- Thoroughly break up the soil.
- Place the shrub in the hole and untangle any roots that have circled the container.
- Fill the hole with soil and water thoroughly.
- Mulch with several inches of pine straw or fine pine bark.

Watering
- Water to keep the soil moist around young plants.
- Older plants can tolerate some dryness but grow and bloom better if regularly watered.

Fertilizing
- Feed in spring and late summer with 1 tablespoon of 10-10-10 fertilizer for each foot of plant height.

Easy Tip

Like its witchhazel relatives, loropetalum's branches also force easily indoors in late winter.

Suggestions for Vigorous Growth
- Maintain mulch year-round, but do not pile it against the trunk.
- Damage may occur at 0 to 5 degrees Fahrenheit—if so, wait to see whether leaves and stems regrow, and then prune as needed.
- Prune to maintain a graceful shape—do *not* lop off the top of the plant.

Pest Control
- No pests or diseases bother this shrub.

Complementary Plants
- Plant against an evergreen backdrop to show off the foliage.
- For a nice effect, use in gardens with a red theme.

Recommended Selections
- 'Burgundy' has bronze-purple leaves with dark-pink flowers.
- 'Blush' has light-pink foliage and pink flowers.
- 'Plum Delight'™, 'Razzle Dazzle', and 'Hines Purpleleaf' are widely available.
- 'Zhuzhou Fuchsia' is good for the colder parts of Georgia.

Mister Lincoln Rose

Rosa 'Mister Lincoln'

A Classic Hybrid Tea Rose Good for Georgia

Despite the fact that hybrid tea roses in Georgia can require spraying every seven to ten days, along with frequent fertilizing and deadheading, growing them can be rewarding. 'Mister Lincoln' has strong stems, urn-shaped buds, and large cupped flowers with up to thirty-five petals that make it ideal for cutting. This hybrid tea is the classic red rose. Its dark, leathery foliage and vigorous habit make it one of the better hybrid teas for Georgia gardens.

Top Reasons to Plant

○ Unsurpassed cutting flower
○ Beautiful red blooms
○ Outstanding fragrance

Useful Hint

Before choosing hybrid tea roses for your garden, get in touch with your local rose society, botanic garden, or other experts to find out which roses perform best in your area.

Bloom Color
Red

Bloom Period
Spring through fall

Height/Width
5 feet x 2 to 3 feet

Planting Location
- Well-drained, fertile, moist soil with lots of organic matter
- Sun

Planting
- Plant bare-root roses during their dormant season.
- Plant containerized roses in early spring or early fall.
- Dig the hole 24 inches wide and as deep as the plant's roots.
- Amend the soil so it is one-third original soil, one-third coarse sand, and one-third organic matter.
- Place the plant in the hole—for bare-root roses, place the roots over a small mound of soil to allow them to spread in all directions.
- Water thoroughly.
- Fill the hole with soil, packing it firmly around the roots, and water again.
- Mulch with pine straw or wood chips.

Watering
- Provide an inch of water each week if there hasn't been that amount of rainfall.
- Water deeply, preferably using a soaker hose.

Fertilizing
- Apply rose fertilizer regularly using label directions.

Easy Tip
If you're not prepared to do the work required for success with hybrid tea roses, explore some other choices, such as landscape roses or old species roses.

Suggestions for Vigorous Growth
- Top-dress with mulch two or three times each year to provide additional organic matter and to help keep roots cool and moist.
- Prune canes in early spring to a height of four to six buds from the base of the previous year's growth.

Pest Control
- Consult your Extension Agent for detailed advice on a spray program for hybrid tea roses.

Complementary Plants
- Plant low-growing perennials such as hardy geraniums or ground covers to help hide the ugly "knees" that so many hybrid teas develop.

Recommended Selections
- Other hybrid teas that do well in Georgia are 'Dolly Parton', with fragrant orange and orange-red flowers measuring 6 to 7 inches across, and 'New Zealand', a bushy, disease-resistant selection with pink-orange flowers.

Mountain Laurel
Kalmia latifolia

A Handsome Native Evergreen with Showy Spring Blooms

Mountain laurel is a tall, exceptionally handsome, evergreen shrub with shiny, leathery leaves that make beautiful holiday roping. In mid- to late spring, mountain laurel bears clusters of white, pink, or red variegated cup-shaped florets. The blooms of the native species you encounter in the mountains are pale-pink, but the modern hybrids are considerably showier, blooming in brighter pinks, reds, and bicolors.

Top Reasons to Plant

○ Beautiful clusters of spring flowers
○ Handsome, leathery evergreen leaves
○ Thrives in partial shade or shade
○ Few pests and diseases
○ Good cut flower and foliage
○ Excellent naturalized in woodland setting

Useful Hint

Caution: Every part of the mountain laurel is poisonous to humans but not to wildlife—though mountain laurel is deer resistant, Bambi will still nibble it.

Bloom Color
White, pink, red, or bicolors

Bloom Period
Spring

Height/Width
7 to 8 feet x 5 to 6 feet

Planting Location
- Rich, moist, well-drained soil with lots of organic matter
- Partial shade or shade

Planting
- Plant in early spring or early fall.
- Dig the hole three times as wide as and slightly shallower than the rootball.
- Add compost or finely shredded bark to the planting hole and the pile of soil.
- Place the shrub in the hole and fill the hole with soil.
- Water thoroughly.
- Mulch with several inches of pine straw or fine pine bark.

Watering
- Water regularly until the plant becomes established if rainfall measures less than an inch per week.
- Once the shrub is established, water deeply during dry spells.

Fertilizing
- Feed in spring with a slow-release fertilizer for shrubs.

Suggestions for Vigorous Growth
- Keep mulched year-round to conserve moisture and to provide gentle feeding as the mulch decays.
- Remove flower heads as they fade.

Easy Tip
If mountain laurel's leaves turn yellowish, with veins remaining green, it probably has chlorosis from inadequate acidity in the soil—use a powdered garden sulfur according to label directions to increase the soil's acidity.

- No pruning is needed—mountain laurel recovers slowly from pruning.

Pest Control
- Few pests and diseases bother this shrub if it's in an appropriate spot.
- Plants grown in the sun are subject to serious leaf disease and insect damage.

Complementary Plants
- Plant at the back of shaded shrub borders.
- Use for naturalizing with rhododendrons and azaleas at the edge of an open woodland.
- Mass on a shady bank for an excellent effect.

Recommended Selections
- 'Ostbo Red' has intense crimson buds opening to pink.
- 'Bullseye' is one of several forms with flowers banded in red inside.
- 'Elf' is a slow-growing, smaller cultivar eventually reaching 4 to 6 feet tall with light-pink buds opening to white.

Nandina

Nandina domestica

A Shade-Tolerant Beauty with Great Berries

Nandina offers wonderful textural relief in a group of other shrubs. In December, it produces an abundant and attractive crop of red berries set against its bamboolike foliage and stems. One of the most shade-tolerant shrubs, nandina can be used as a foundation shrub or as a screen plant. The introduction of dwarf cultivars, particularly those with red foliage, has made nandina a shrub sought after by many gardeners.

Top Reasons to Plant

- Beautiful, showy clusters of red berries
- Delicate, airy foliage
- Bamboolike appearance
- Evergreen foliage
- Thrives in shade
- Mounded, small habit
- Fiery autumn leaves
- Tolerates sun

Bloom Color

White followed by red berries on upright types—dwarf types generally don't bloom or bear berries

Bloom Period

Spring, with berries in fall

Height/Width

$1^1/_2$ to 8 feet x $1^1/_2$ to 5 feet

Planting Location

- Rich, moist, well-drained soil with lots of organic matter
- Shade or partial shade for upright types
- Sun to light shade for dwarf types

Planting

- Plant in fall or spring.
- Dig the hole three times as wide as and slightly shallower than the rootball.
- Thoroughly break up the soil, leaving no large clumps.
- Place the shrub in the hole, making sure it's at the same depth as it was growing.
- Fill the hole with soil and water well.
- Mulch with several inches of pine straw or fine pine bark.

Watering

- Keep the soil moist, if possible, although mature plants can withstand dryness if in shade.

Easy Tip

For the most attractive shape, prune stems of upright types to varying heights.

Fertilizing

- During the first year, feed in March, May, and June with 1 tablespoon of 10-10-10 fertilizer per foot of plant height.
- After the first year, feed in April and June with the same amount of fertilizer.

Suggestions for Vigorous Growth

- Dwarf, mounded types need little pruning—just snip off winter damage.
- Prune out the oldest stems of tall types in March if the plant has grown too large.

Pest Control

- No serious pest or disease problems bother this plant.

Complementary Plants

- Combine tall nandinas with leatherleaf mahonia (*Mahonia bealei*), aucuba, and hydrangea.
- Use mounding nandinas for edging, especially around an evergreen.

Recommended Selections

- 'Gulf Stream'™ is a common dwarf form with brilliant-red leaves in winter.
- 'San Gabriel' grows only 24 inches high and has green "ferny" leaves.

Useful Hint

Nandinas bear heavier crops of berries if several are grouped together—or if at least several are in the neighborhood.

New Dawn Rose

Rosa 'New Dawn'

A Vigorous Climber with Lovely Pink Blooms

'New Dawn' can be seen covering log cabins or rambling over arbors in long-abandoned gardens when you drive the back country roads of Georgia. The flowers hold up well even in the rain, and the canes can grow to 10 feet tall or more in a single season, easily covering an arbor or trellis. 'New Dawn' is a good rose for covering an ugly chain-link fence. Just weave its new shoots in and out of the links.

Top Reasons to Plant

○ Beautiful, showy flowers
○ Fragrant blossoms
○ Extends landscape vertically
○ Good cut flower
○ Attracts butterflies

Useful Hint

Plant 'New Dawn' where it has lots of room to spread—this isn't a plant for a small garden unless you can train it to grow vertically.

Bloom Color
Pink

Bloom Period
Spring

Height/Width
15 to 20 feet x 3 to 6 feet

Planting Location
• Well-drained, fertile soil with lots of organic matter
• Sun, although climbers bloom well with their branches in sun and their roots in shade

Planting
• Plant bare-root roses during the dormant season.
• Plant containerized roses in early spring or early fall.
• Dig the hole 24 inches wide and as deep as the plant's roots.
• Amend the soil so it is one-third original soil, one-third coarse sand, and one-third organic matter.
• Place the plant in the hole—for bare-root roses, place the roots over a small mound of soil to allow them to spread in all directions.
• Water thoroughly.
• Fill the hole with soil, packing it firmly around the roots, and water again.
• Mulch with pine straw or wood chips.

Watering
• Provide an inch of water each week if there hasn't been that amount of rainfall.
• Water deeply, preferably using a soaker hose.

Easy Tip

If your 'New Dawn' is grafted rather than growing on its own roots, plant it so the bud union is at ground level.

Fertilizing
• Apply rose fertilizer regularly using label directions.

Suggestions for Vigorous Growth
• Top-dress with mulch two or three times each year to provide additional organic matter and to help keep roots cool and moist.
• Using twine or stretch ties that expand, train the canes to grow in a fan shape—horizontal rose canes produce more flowers than vertical ones.

Pest Control
• 'New Dawn' resists diseases but is susceptible to blackspot—check with your Extension Agent or garden center about controls that work well in your area.

Complementary Plants
• Underplant with catmint, lavender, or other bushy companions to hide this climbing rose's bare legs.

Recommended Selections
• 'White Dawn' is very similar to 'New Dawn' but has white flowers.

Oakleaf Hydrangea

Hydrangea quercifolia

The Queen of the Shade-Loving Shrubs

Gardeners may exclaim over the large white blooms of an oakleaf hydrangea in June, but they often forget that its leaf color rivals the maples in autumn. They might also forget that beneath the green leaves, thick branches with peeling bark prove striking in winter. A single oakleaf hydrangea is attractive in a small landscape, but if space is available, it's best used in a shrub border or a mass planting.

Top Reasons to Plant

- Beautiful, huge summer blooms
- Large, tropical-looking leaves
- Striking bark in winter
- Thrives in shade
- Disease and pest resistant
- Excellent for beginning gardeners
- Good cut or dried flower

Useful Hint

If oakleaf hydrangea's big leaves wilt, don't despair—if you water right away, the plant usually perks right up.

Bloom Color
White fading to purple then brown

Bloom Period
Summer

Height/Width
4 to 6 feet x 5 to 8 feet

Planting Location
- Rich, moist, well-drained soil with lots of organic matter
- Partial sun to shade

Planting
- Plant in spring.
- Dig the hole five times as wide as and slightly shallower than the rootball.
- Mix the soil from the hole with an equal amount of soil conditioner or compost.
- Place the shrub in the hole and fill the hole with soil.
- Water thoroughly.
- Mulch with several inches of pine straw or fine pine bark.

Watering
- Regular watering is essential, but root rot will occur if it's planted where water pools frequently.
- Watch for signs of wilting—that means water immediately!

Fertilizing
- During the first year, feed in March, June, and August with 1 tablespoon of 10-10-10 fertilizer per foot of plant height.
- After the first year, feed in March and June using the same amount of fertilizer.

Easy Tip
Like all hydrangeas, oakleaf hydrangea loves water, so plant it where it's convenient to the hose.

Suggestions for Vigorous Growth
- Keep mulched year-round.
- In late June, prune if needed.
- On established plants, remove the oldest branches every year.
- Cut back spent blooms in winter after they deteriorate.

Pest Control
- No serious pests or diseases trouble this plant.

Complementary Plants
- Use in a mixed-shrub border in shade.
- Plant compact cultivars in smaller gardens.
- Plant along the edge of a woodland.

Recommended Selections
- 'Snow Queen' has huge, dense white flowers held erect above its foliage.
- 'Pee Wee' grows only 3 to 4 feet tall.

Pieris

Pieris japonica

A Harbinger of Spring with Cascading Clusters of Blossoms

Whether you know it as andromeda or pieris, this mounding shrub has chains of lightly fragrant spring flowers cascading over the plant's spreading branches. Its reddish bronze new growth unfurls into lustrous evergreen foliage. A common name for pieris is lily-of-the-valley shrub, as the tiny flowers resemble those of the popular ground cover. This durable and truly beautiful shrub begins blooming before winter passes and is a favorite harbinger of spring.

Top Reasons to Plant

- Beautiful chains of flowers in late winter
- Fragrant blossoms
- Lustrous green foliage
- Showy new leaves of reddish bronze
- Excellent with azaleas and rhododendrons
- Thrives in partial shade

Useful Hint

Pieris is a relative of rhododendrons and azaleas—it both looks good and grows well with them.

Bloom Color
White or pink

Bloom Period
Late winter

Height/Width
4 to 6 feet x 4 to 6 feet

Planting Location
- Moist, acidic, well-drained soil with lots of organic matter
- Partial shade

Planting
- Plant in early fall or spring.
- Dig the hole five times as wide as and slightly shallower than the rootball.
- Add compost or finely shredded bark to the planting hole and the pile of soil.
- Place the shrub in the hole and fill the hole with soil.
- Water thoroughly.
- Mulch with several inches of pine straw or fine pine bark.

Watering
- Do not let the soil dry out.
- Keep the soil moist for the first three summer seasons.
- After that, water weekly when there hasn't been an inch of rainfall.

Fertilizing
- In early April, feed with a fertilizer for acid-loving plants, such as an azalea-camellia fertilizer.

Easy Tip
In heavy clay soils, consider growing pieris in a raised bed.

Suggestions for Vigorous Growth
- Prune to shape or to remove dead branches.
- Cut back individual stems immediately after flowering in spring.
- Excessive watering and poor soil drainage can cause root rot.

Pest Control
- If twig dieback appears, prune out affected stems immediately.
- Lace bugs can be a problem—if they are, control them with an insecticide in mid-April and August.

Complementary Plants
- Mix with azaleas, rhododendrons, and ground covers.
- Plant at the edge of a woodland for an excellent effect.
- Use as specimen shrubs near the front door.

Recommended Selections
- 'Variegata' has year-round interest because of its white-edged leaves.
- 'Compacta' grows 4 to 6 feet tall and blooms heavily.

Plumleaf Azalea

Rhododendron prunifolium

A Georgia Gem with Summer Blooms

In July and August, when there are few blooms on other shrubs, plumleaf azalea presents bright-red flowers on glossy green foliage. Native to west Georgia, it is found around Callaway Gardens, lining the streams meandering down from Pine Mountain. The best use of plumleaf azalea is beneath tall pines and hardwoods, where little but English ivy and scraggly underbrush grows.

Top Reasons to Plant

- Beautiful summer flowers
- Attractive foliage
- Easy to grow
- Few pests and diseases

Useful Hint

This is the signature plant of Callaway Gardens, which contains extensive plantings worth a special trip to view.

Bloom Color
Red

Bloom Period
Summer

Height/Width
7 to 10 feet x 6 to 8 feet

Planting Location
- Rich, moist, well-drained soil
- Partial sun, with afternoon shade essential

Planting
- Plant in early fall.
- Dig the hole 5 feet wide and as deep as the rootball.
- Mix 4 cubic feet of soil conditioner with the soil from the hole.
- Place the plant in the hole and untangle any roots circling the container.
- Set the plant at the same depth it was growing.
- Water thoroughly.
- Mulch heavily with pine straw starting 3 inches away from the stem.

Watering
- Water weekly, especially in hot weather and drought.

Fertilizing
- During the first year, feed in March, June, and August with 1 tablespoon of 10-10-10 fertilizer per foot of plant height.
- After the first year, feed in March and June using 2 tablespoons of 10-10-10 per foot of plant height.

Easy Tip

Plumleaf azalea forms an attractive shape naturally, so little pruning is required.

Suggestions for Vigorous Growth
- Prune any time to remove dead wood.
- Buds for next year's flowers form in summer, so pruning at any time during the year will reduce blooms in the current year or the following summer.
- Keep mulched year-round.

Pest Control
- Few pests and diseases trouble this plant.

Complementary Plants
- Combine with Christmas fern (*Polystichum acrostichoides*), wild ginger (*Asarum shuttleworthii*), and a few summersweets (*Clethra alnifolia*) to create an enticing garden area.
- Try planting trumpet creeper (*Campsis radicans*) and cross vine (*Anisostichus* [*Bignonia*] *capreolata*) nearby for a great butterfly and hummingbird retreat.

Recommended Selections
- 'Cherry Bomb' is orange-red, and 'Peach Glow' is orange-pink.

Prague Viburnum

Viburnum × pragense

One of the Best Viburnums for the South

If you're looking for an indestructible evergreen shrub, Prague viburnum is it. While it lacks the fabulous scent of Koreanspice viburnum, Prague viburnum has outstanding flowers and berries. The flower buds, borne in flat clusters, are pink when they appear in April and turn white after opening. The berries are red, but change gradually to black by late October. You have to be quick to see them—birds love them!

Top Reasons to Plant

○ Beautiful blooms
○ Showy berries
○ Attracts butterflies and birds
○ Needs little maintenance
○ Few pests and diseases

Useful Hint

Prague viburnum is almost as hardy as Burford holly, but it isn't used enough in Georgia landscapes.

Bloom Color
White

Bloom Period
Spring

Height/Width
8 to 12 feet x 8 to 10 feet

Planting Location
- Prefers slightly acidic, moist, well-drained soil with lots of organic matter but tolerates wide variety of soils
- Sun or partial shade

Planting
- Plant in late fall or early spring.
- Dig the hole five times as wide as and slightly shallower than the rootball.
- If the soil is clay, mix in 2 cubic feet of soil conditioner or compost.
- Place the plant in the hole and pack the hole with soil.
- Water thoroughly.
- Mulch with several inches of pine straw or fine pine bark.

Watering
- Water occasionally for the first month.
- Water during the heat of summer for the first two years—thereafter, unless it's on a hot, dry site, it may not require watering.

Easy Tip

Prague viburnum is one of the "best of the best" green screens for the South.

Fertilizing
- Feed in March, June, and August with 1 tablespoon of 10-10-10 fertilizer per foot of plant height.

Suggestions for Vigorous Growth
- Prune if required just after flowering.

Pest Control
- This plant has many potential pests, but they're fairly rare.

Complementary Plants
- Use as a backdrop for blooming perennials.
- Plant with Japanese anemone (*Anemone japonica*) and lantana (*Lantana camara*).

Recommended Selections
- Koreanspice viburnum (*V. carlesii*) can spice up a neighborhood with its sweet scent in March.
- Snowball viburnum (*V. macrocephalum*) has large, round, white flower heads in early May remarkably similar to those on a hydrangea.

Purple Beautyberry

Callicarpa dichotoma

A Stunner with Lavender-Purple Berries in Fall

Purple beautyberry, with its screaming purple berries, is eye-catching in fall, all the more so because it's nondescript the rest of the year. The tiny pink flowers are hidden by the leaves in summer. The individual berries that follow are only 1/4 inch in diameter, but they grow in 1-inch clusters up and down multiple gray stems. Mockingbirds and brown thrashers love the fruits and consume most of them by late fall.

Top Reasons to Plant

○ Showy purple berries late summer and fall
○ Attracts butterflies and birds
○ Few insects and diseases
○ Naturalizes well
○ Likes average soil

Useful Hint

The native American beautyberry (*Callicarpa americana*) has rather coarse leaves and is not as attractive as purple beautyberry.

Bloom Color
Pink flowers followed by purple fruits

Bloom Period
Summer, with berries in fall

Height/Width
4 to 5 feet x 4 to 5 feet

Planting Location
- Prefers moist, well-drained soil but is adaptable
- Sun to partial sun—full sun is best for berry production

Planting
- Plant in fall or early spring.
- Dig the hole three times as wide as and slightly shallower than the rootball.
- Thoroughly break up the soil.
- Place the plant in the hole, untangling the roots if necessary.
- Set the plant at the same depth it was growing and fill the hole with soil.
- Water thoroughly.
- Mulch with pine straw.

Watering
- After beautyberry is established, it rarely needs watering.

Fertilizing
- Feed in April and August with 1 tablespoon of 10-10-10 fertilizer per foot of plant height.

Easy Tip
If the top of the beautyberry plant is killed in a severe winter, it grows back from the roots the following spring.

Suggestions for Vigorous Growth
- Cut out dead stems in late winter or early spring.
- To encourage new growth with lots of flowers and berries, prune in early March to half the height you want the shrub to grow.
- Any overgrown beautyberry may be cut back to 1 foot tall in early spring and allowed to regrow.

Pest Control
- No serious insects or diseases trouble beautyberry.

Complementary Plants
- Plant in front of evergreen shrubs that will provide a backdrop to the fall berries—dwarf Burford holly, camellia, or English laurel are all good choices.
- Put in a row or large mass at the base of tall trees, such as pines.

Recommended Selections
- *Callicarpa dichotoma* 'Albifructus' has white berries instead of purple.

Purple Japanese Barberry

Berberis thunbergii 'Atropurpurea'

A Reliable Red-Leafed Shrub for a Sunny Spot

Purple Japanese barberry is a favorite of landscape professionals because of its reliable purple to red foliage, offering a nice contrast in green landscapes. Its color holds throughout the summer as long as it's in sun, then in fall the leaves change to deep-amber. Over winter, the thorny thicket adds texture to the garden. Adaptable to most soils and summer drought, resistant to pests and diseases, Japanese barberry couldn't be easier to grow.

Top Reasons to Plant

- Reddish purple foliage all summer
- Tolerates heat and humidity
- Resistant to pests and diseases
- Withstands drought
- Adjusts to a variety of soil types
- Interesting winter texture

Useful Hint

Japanese barberry has spiny leaves and thorns, so be sure to wear gloves when working with it.

Bloom Color
Inconspicuous yellow flowers

Bloom Period
Spring

Height/Width
2 to 3 feet x 3 to 5 feet

Planting Location
- Prefers slightly acidic, well-drained, loose soil, but adapts to most soils
- Sun

Planting
- Plant bare-root stock in early spring.
- Plant containerized stock anytime during the growing season.
- Dig the hole three times as wide as and slightly shallower than the rootball.
- Thoroughly break up the soil.
- Place the shrub in the hole and fill the hole with soil.
- Water thoroughly.
- Mulch with several inches of pine straw or fine pine bark.

Watering
- During the first year, water every two weeks in spring and fall, and every seven to ten days in summer.
- Once established, this plant tolerates drought.

Fertilizing
- In early spring, feed with a slow-release fertilizer for acid-loving plants.

Easy Tip
Japanese barberry tolerates drought, urban pollution, and neglect, so it's hard to beat for a low-maintenance plant.

Suggestions for Vigorous Growth
- Maintain mulch year-round.
- Prune to shape in late winter.
- Overgrown shrubs can be cut back to 10 inches in early spring to rejuvenate the plant.
- Root rot is a problem in wet soils.

Pest Control
- No serious diseases or insects bother this plant.

Complementary Plants
- Use as a specimen in otherwise green plantings.
- Plant as a low border or hedge to deter pets and wildlife.

Recommended Selections
- The low-growing 'Crimson Pygmy' reaches only 3 feet high at maturity.
- 'Rose Glow' has excellent reddish purple foliage and is a bit larger.

Rhododendron

Rhododendron species

A Gorgeous Spring Bloomer Perfect for Georgia

Only in the Pacific Northwest do rhododendrons prosper the way they do in Georgia. The massive spring displays at Callaway Gardens are famous around the world. With a bit of soil preparation, your landscape can have the same stunning effect. This grand lady of the April landscape bears flowers from pure-white to yellow, orange, pink, red, and lavender. If you find yourself planting more than four, you might be on the way to rhodo addiction!

Top Reasons to Plant

- Beautiful clusters of spring blooms
- Handsome evergreen foliage
- Thrives anywhere in Georgia if sited correctly
- Few pests and diseases if cared for properly
- Outstanding in woodland settings with high shade

Useful Hint

Rhododendrons are *not* full-shade plants—they must have at least a half-day's sun to bloom well.

Bloom Color
White, pink, red, orange, lavender, or yellow

Bloom Period
April

Height/Width
4 to 15 feet x 4 to 15 feet

Planting Location
- Well-drained, acidic soil with lots of organic matter
- Sun at least half the day, with morning sun and afternoon shade

Planting
- Plant in early spring.
- Dig the hole five times as wide as (at least 4 feet) and slightly shallower than the rootball.
- Remove one-third of the native soil, and add to it 4 cubic feet of compost or soil conditioner.
- Mix everything together to make a raised mound in which to plant.
- Take the plant out of its pot, and use a sharp knife inserted halfway down the side of the rootball to cut through the roots down to the bottom.
- Place the plant in the mound, flaring roots out in all directions, and pack soil on top of the roots.
- Water thoroughly.
- Mulch with several inches of pine straw or fine pine bark, keeping the mulch 3 inches away from the stem.

Watering
- Water weekly if rainfall hasn't totaled an inch, especially in hot weather.

Easy Tip
If you have heavy-clay soil, you may plant rhododendrons in raised beds and prepare to water and feed them regularly—these plants don't tolerate poor drainage.

Fertilizing
- Feed with 1 tablespoon of 10-10-10 fertilizer per foot of plant height in spring and again in midsummer.

Suggestions for Vigorous Growth
- Trim off winter damage in spring.
- Prune lightly each year after blooming to shape plant.

Pest Control
- If properly planted and cared for, this plant has few pests and diseases.

Complementary Plants
- Make rhododendrons the centerpiece of a woodland garden by surrounding them with ferns, toad lilies, Solomon's seal, and camellias.

Recommended Selections
- 'Scintillation' has light-pink flowers and tolerates Georgia heat.
- 'Ramapo' grows only 2 feet tall and has violet-purple flowers.
- *Rhododendron catawbiense* 'Nova Zembla' grows 8 feet tall and has large red flowers.

Rose of Sharon
Hibiscus syriacus

An Old-Fashioned Favorite with Late-Summer Flowers

Rose of Sharon is one of those "pass-along plants" that some believe has passed itself along a little too often. The shrub is legendarily prolific, rivaling privet with its ability to seed and grow on unused land. And its growth is unkempt however you prune, plus the winter seed capsules are ugly. But the multitudes of summer flowers on this tough plant cause all negative thoughts about it to vanish.

Top Reasons to Plant

- Blooms in late summer when few other shrubs do
- Attracts butterflies and hummingbirds
- Blooms on new growth so it can be pruned severely
- Inexpensive hedge or screen
- Drought tolerant when established

Useful Hint

If you plant one of the truly old-fashioned types of rose of Sharon, rather than one of the new seedless cultivars, be prepared to pull up *lots* of unwanted seedlings every spring.

Bloom Color
White, pink, lavender-blue, lilac, or deep-red

Bloom Period
July to September

Height/Width
5 to 12 feet x 5 to 8 feet

Planting Location
- Prefers well-drained soil with lots of organic matter
- Sun

Planting
- Plant in early spring or early fall.
- Dig the hole three times as wide as and slightly more shallow than the rootball.
- Thoroughly break up the soil, leaving no large clumps.
- Place the plant in the hole and untangle any roots that have circled the container.
- Fill the hole with soil.
- Water thoroughly.
- Mulch with several inches of pine straw or fine pine bark.

Watering
- During the first four weeks, keep the soil evenly moist.
- Once the plant becomes established, water only during prolonged dry spells.

Fertilizing
- Feed with 1 tablespoon of 10-10-10 fertilizer per foot of height in spring and again in midsummer.

Easy Tip
Rose of Sharon blooms may be single, semidouble, or double—buy a plant in bloom to ensure you get the form you prefer.

Suggestions for Vigorous Growth
- Prune heavily in winter, cutting back branches to a pair of outward-facing buds.
- To control height on a mature plant, prune severely.
- For a treelike form, prune lower branches away from trunks.

Pest Control
- Rose of Sharon attracts Japanese beetles, which may devour leaves—consult your Extension Agent or garden center for controls.

Complementary Plants
- Use against a bare garage wall for beauty during the summer.
- Underplant tree forms with annuals, perennials, or spreading hollies.

Recommended Selections
- 'Diana' has solid white blossoms and produces no seedlings.
- 'Blue Bird' has lavender-blue flowers.
- 'Minerva', 'Aphrodite', and 'Helene' are all outstanding National Arboretum introductions that are sterile (produce no seedlings).

Smokebush

Cotinus coggygria

A Showy Performer with Big Billowing Blooms

Imagine a shrub that looks as if it's surrounded by hazy smoke in the late afternoon June sunshine. That's the visual effect of smokebush. The flower stems, covered in silky hair, give the shrub its smoky look from June until September. Purple-leafed forms have become more available in recent years than those with green leaves. Some fade to green as summer progresses, but a few keep their purple leaves until fall.

Top Reasons to Plant

○ Gorgeous, airy plumes of blossoms
○ Long-lasting effect
○ Striking fall foliage
○ Few insects or diseases
○ Grows well in poor, rocky soil
○ Requires little maintenance

Useful Hint

If you prefer smokebush with reddish purple foliage, buy plants in mid- to late summer—some fade to green late in the season.

Bloom Color
Yellowish, turning to pink and purple

Bloom Period
Late spring, with "smoke" developing in early summer

Height/Width
8 to 12 feet x 8 to 12 feet

Planting Location
- Prefers loose, fast-draining soil, so it's ideal for poor, rocky ground— tolerates any soil except wet ones
- Sun

Planting
- Plant in spring or fall.
- Dig the hole three times as wide as and slightly shallower than the rootball.
- Thoroughly break up the soil.
- If the roots are densely wound around inside the container, use a sharp knife to make two slits on opposite sides of the rootball, starting halfway down and continuing to the bottom.
- Spread the roots apart and place the plant in the hole.
- Keeping the roots spread apart, fill the hole with soil.
- Water thoroughly.
- Mulch with several inches of pine straw or pine chips.

Watering
- Keep the soil evenly moist when the plant is young.
- Mature plants can tolerate drier soil— but water during hot, dry summers.

Easy Tip

Smokebush leafs out late, so don't be concerned that it has died over winter if it has no leaves after other shrubs do.

Fertilizing
- During the first year, feed in March, June, and August with 1 tablespoon of 10-10-10 fertilizer per foot of plant height.
- After the first year, feed in April and June using the same amount of fertilizer.

Suggestions for Vigorous Growth
- Little pruning is necessary—or desirable.
- Trim any straggly stems in early spring.

Pest Control
- Occasionally examine the stems and undersides of leaves for small white scale insects—if you find them, ask your Extension Agent about effective controls.

Complementary Plants
- Use as a specimen shrub—site it where it can be admired.
- Plant as the centerpiece of a flower border surrounded by plants with silvery foliage and pink or purple blooms.

Recommended Selections
- 'Royal Purple' is the most common purple-leafed cultivar, with purple-red smoke.
- 'Daydream' has dense branches, green leaves, and pink smoke.

91

Spring-Flowering Azalea

Rhododendron species

A Southern Classic Beloved by Millions

Who can forget the stunning shades of white, pink, red, and lavender that grace the cities and suburbs of Georgia in April? Combined with the clouds of pure-white dogwood blooms that hang overhead, the sight is enough to make a Northern visitor pull up stakes and move south. There are both evergreen and deciduous azaleas. Centuries of hybridization and wide availability mean there's a distinctive azalea within everyone's reach.

Top Reasons to Plant

- Brilliant display of spring flowers
- Evergreen foliage on many types
- Thrives in shade
- Good for cutting

Useful Hint

Select your azaleas carefully to ensure their colors are attractive with your house and with one another.

Bloom Color
Shades of red, pink, lavender, white, salmon, or variegated

Bloom Period
Spring

Height/Width
2 to 8 feet x 4 to 10 feet

Planting Location
- Rich, moist, well-drained soil amended with lots of organic matter
- Afternoon shade a must

Planting
- Plant in fall or spring.
- Dig the hole 5 feet wide and slightly shallower than the rootball.
- Mix 4 cubic feet of soil conditioner with the soil from the hole, creating a mound.
- Untangle any roots that have circled the container and place the plant in the mound at the same height it was growing.
- Pack soil around the roots and water thoroughly.
- Mulch with several inches of pine straw, keeping mulch 3 inches away from the stem.

Watering
- Never allow azaleas to dry out.
- Water weekly when rainfall hasn't totaled an inch.

Fertilizing
- During the first year, feed in March, June, and August with 1 tablespoon of 10-10-10 fertilizer per foot of plant height.

Easy Tip
Use wide plastic garbage bag ties to attach tags with the variety's name to the lower branches of your azaleas.

- After the first year, feed in April and June with 2 tablespoons of 10-10-10 per foot of plant height.

Suggestions for Vigorous Growth
- Maintain 3 inches of mulch year-round to hold moisture and provide protection from cold.
- Prune right after plants stop blooming.

Pest Control
- In dry years, spider mites may occur— consult the Extension Service for controls.
- Lace bugs are a frequent problem in warm weather—consult the Extension Service for controls.

Complementary Plants
- Pair with dogwoods for a beautiful effect.
- Combine with other evergreens to avoid the monotony of a single-leaf texture.

Recommended Selections
- Glenn Dale, Robin Hill, and Girard hybrids are a few of the many you will find.
- Exbury azaleas are a common deciduous type.

Summersweet

Clethra alnifolia

A Very Fragrant Bloomer That's Adaptable to Boot

Summersweet is prized for its white summer blooms at a time when only perennials seem brave enough to face the heat. The individual flowers are small, but hundreds of them line each flower stem, resembling a bottlebrush. A shrub will be covered with multitudes of these 6-inch flower spikes in midsummer. The sweet scent spreading throughout a garden attracts butterflies and bees. And the deep-green spring leaves turn vivid yellow in autumn.

Top Reasons to Plant

- Fragrant, pretty blossoms
- Excellent fall color
- Thrives in partial shade to sun
- Tolerates moist soil
- Few pests and diseases
- Easy to grow

Useful Hint

Summersweet flowers are so fragrant that just one or two plants can perfume a whole garden.

Bloom Color
White

Bloom Period
Mid- to late summer

Height/Width
4 to 8 feet x 4 to 6 feet

Planting Location
- Moist, acidic soil with plenty of organic matter
- Sun to shade

Planting
- Plant in fall or spring.
- Dig the hole three times as wide as and slightly deeper than the rootball.
- Mix at least 1 cubic foot of soil conditioner with the soil removed from the hole.
- Place the plant in the hole $1/2$ inch deeper than it was growing.
- Fill the hole with soil, and water thoroughly.
- Mulch with several inches of pine straw, keeping the mulch 3 inches away from the stem.

Watering
- Water regularly for best performance and the most flowers.
- Do not let the soil dry out.

Fertilizing
- During the first year, feed in March, June, and August with 1 tablespoon of 10-10-10 fertilizer per foot of plant height.
- After the first year, feed in April using the same amount of fertilizer.

Easy Tip

Summersweet thrives in swamps and on stream banks, so it's a wonderful plant to adorn a landscape pond.

Suggestions for Vigorous Growth
- Prune in late winter before new growth begins—this plant flowers on new growth.
- Little pruning is usually required, but if the plant has grown too large for its spot, cut back one-fourth of its stems to the ground each year for four years.
- Summersweet spreads by rhizomes (fleshy roots) and suckers—remove unwanted plants anytime.

Pest Control
- Few insects or diseases bother this plant.

Complementary Plants
- Plant with lantana and Mexican heather to attract additional pollinating insects.
- Combine with evergreen azaleas on the shady side of a house where nothing seems to grow well.

Recommended Selections
- 'Hummingbird', a dwarf selection, has large white flowers with deep-green summer leaves turning clear-yellow in fall.
- 'Rosea' has pink flowers.

Sun Flare Rose

Rosa 'Sun Flare'

A Delightful, Easy-Care, Long-Blooming Yellow Rose

'Sun Flare' has clusters of delicately scented blooms that start out golden-yellow and fade as they open. This delightful rose provides a good transition in the flower garden between bright colors, and it can extend the blooming season in the shrub border. It bears a profusion of blooms with three to twelve per cluster from spring until frost. And 'Sun Flare' resists diseases so well that it doesn't require regular spraying.

Top Reasons to Plant

- Beautiful flowers
- Fragrant blossoms
- Disease resistant
- Requires little care compared to many other roses
- Works well in mixed borders with perennials and other shrubs
- Good cut flower

Useful Hint

'Sun Flare' is a floribunda rose, a group that produces lots of flowers on vigorous, bushy plants.

Bloom Color
Yellow

Bloom Period
Spring to frost

Height/Width
3 to 4 feet x 3 to 4 feet

Planting Location
- Deep, moist, well-drained soil with lots of organic matter
- Sun

Planting
- Plant bare-root roses during their dormant season as soon as you get them.
- Plant containerized roses in early spring or early fall.
- Dig the hole 24 inches wide and as deep as the plant's roots.
- Amend the soil so it is one-third original soil, one-third coarse sand, and one-third organic matter (compost, composted manure, or composted pine bark).
- Place the plant in the hole—for bare-root roses, place the roots over a small mound of soil to allow them to spread in all directions.
- Water thoroughly.
- Fill the hole with soil, packing it firmly around the roots, and water again.
- Mulch with pine straw or wood chips.

Watering
- Provide an inch of water each week if there hasn't been that amount of rainfall.
- Water deeply, preferably using a soaker hose.

Easy Tip

This is an excellent choice for a rose-lover who doesn't want to spray every week.

Fertilizing
- Apply rose fertilizer regularly using label directions.

Suggestions for Vigorous Growth
- Top-dress with mulch two or three times each year to provide additional organic matter and to help keep roots cool and moist.
- Prune in early spring just as buds are swelling, cutting back to five or seven buds from the base and removing any damaged or dead wood.

Pest Control
- 'Sun Flare' doesn't require spraying on a regular basis.

Complementary Plants
- Plant in the flower garden with perennials and annuals.
- Mix into the shrub border to extend blooming beyond spring.

Recommended Selections
- 'Betty Prior' is another excellent floribunda rose—it has bright-pink, single flowers and is a good repeat bloomer.

The Sweetheart Rose

Rosa 'Cécile Brunner'

A Charming Pink Rose Needing Little Care

The buds of 'Cécile Brunner' are like those of hybrid teas, but the sweetheart rose doesn't have the problems of hybrid teas. It often shows up in old, well-established gardens where it thrives with little or no care. This delightful, disease-resistant rose tolerates poor soil and partial shade. From mid-spring until frost, sprays of up to twelve flowers appear, perfuming the air with a heady scent. The foliage looks good even without spraying.

Top Reasons to Plant

- Beautiful flowers
- Fragrant blossoms
- Disease resistant
- Requires little care compared to many other roses
- Works well in mixed borders with perennials and other shrubs
- Good cut flower

Useful Hint

Like many old-fashioned roses, 'Cécile Brunner' requires little pruning, so you can restrict your work to cutting flowers.

Bloom Color
Creamy pink with salmon center

Bloom Period
Spring to frost

Height/Width
3 to 4 feet x 3 to 4 feet

Planting Location
- Deep, moist, well-drained soil with lots of organic matter
- Sun
- Good air circulation

Planting
- Plant bare-root roses during their dormant season as soon as you get them.
- Plant containerized roses in early spring or early fall.
- Dig the hole 24 inches wide and as deep as the plant's roots.
- Amend the soil so it is one-third original soil, one-third coarse sand, and one-third organic matter (compost, composted manure, or composted pine bark).
- Place the plant in the hole—for bare-root roses, place the roots over a small mound of soil to allow them to spread in all directions.
- Water thoroughly.
- Fill the hole with soil, packing it firmly around the roots, and water again.
- Mulch with pine straw or wood chips.

Watering
- Provide an inch of water each week if there hasn't been that amount of rainfall.
- Water deeply, preferably using a soaker hose.

Easy Tip
Good air circulation reduces the threat of diseases such as powdery mildew and blackspot.

Fertilizing
- Apply rose fertilizer regularly using label directions.

Suggestions for Vigorous Growth
- Top-dress with mulch two or three times each year to provide additional organic matter and to help keep roots cool and moist.
- Prune only to remove dead or damaged wood or to lightly shape the plant.

Pest Control
- 'Cécile Brunner' doesn't require spraying on a regular basis.

Complementary Plants
- Plant in the flower garden with perennials and annuals.
- Mix into the shrub border to extend blooming beyond spring.

Recommended Selections
- A climbing form of 'Cécile Brunner' is also available—it grows from 15 to 20 feet tall but doesn't rebloom as the shrub variety does.

Sweetshrub

Calycanthus floridus

An Incredibly Fragrant Bloomer with Good Fall Color

This native plant grows well in all but the sandiest, driest parts of Georgia. Its reddish maroon flowers appear in May and are variously described as "pleasantly fruity" and "a combination of banana, strawberry, and pineapple." The strength of the fragrance definitely varies between plants, so be sure to select one when it's blooming if you want strong fragrance. Sweetshrub sprouts vigorously—plant one, and in a few years, you'll have three or four growing beside it.

Top Reasons to Plant

- Wonderful fragrance
- Pretty spring blooms
- No pests or diseases
- Good fall color
- Tolerates variety of soils
- Thrives in sun to partial shade

Useful Hint

Sprouts of sweetshrub are easy to dig up and transplant or give away as a "pass-along plant."

Bloom Color
Maroon-red

Bloom Period
Midspring into summer

Height/Width
5 to 8 feet x 5 to 8 feet

Planting Location
- Prefers moist, well-drained soil with organic matter, but tolerates average soil of any type
- Full sun to shade

Planting
- Plant in late spring.
- Dig the hole three times as wide as and slightly shallower than the rootball.
- Thoroughly break up the soil, leaving no large clumps.
- Place the shrub in the hole and fill the hole with soil.
- Water thoroughly.
- Mulch with several inches of pine straw or fine pine bark.

Watering
- Keep the soil moist around young shrubs.
- Water deeply in the heat of summer if the leaves become droopy.

Easy Tip
Sweetshrub adapts to everything from full sun to partial shade—if you don't want it to grow too tall, give it full sun.

Fertilizing
- If you want sweetshrub to grow more rapidly, apply 1 tablespoon of 10-10-10 fertilizer per foot of plant height in spring and again in midsummer.

Suggestions for Vigorous Growth
- Prune each year after flowering to avoid a wild, scraggly look.

Pest Control
- No insects or diseases trouble this shrub.

Complementary Plants
- Plant in a border with other shrubs that have varying seasons of interest.
- Place near a driveway or patio to enjoy the fragrance.

Recommended Selections
- 'Athens' has yellow flowers and a powerful fragrance that can permeate a neighborhood.

Weigela

Weigela florida

A Foolproof Member of the Honeysuckle Family

Weigelas are dense-flowering shrubs with spreading branches arching to the ground in maturity. Cousins of the honeysuckle, their gift to the gardener is color late in the year and a disposition to thrive no matter what the conditions. The flowers are showy clusters of inch-long, tubular flowers covering the plant in late spring and early summer. Some have a slight fragrance, and some have repeat blooms later in the season.

Top Reasons to Plant

- Showy clusters of flowers
- Attracts hummingbirds and butterflies
- Blooms after most other spring-flowering shrubs
- Vigorous in most situations
- Graceful, arching form
- Good fall color
- Easy to grow

Bloom Color
Rosy shades of pink and crimson, or white

Bloom Period
Late spring to early summer

Height/Width
3 to 10 feet x 8 to 12 feet

Planting Location
- Well-drained, fertile, moist soil
- Sun for best flowering, but blooms with light shade

Planting
- Plant in spring or fall.
- Dig the hole three times as wide as and slightly shallower than the rootball.
- Thoroughly break up the soil, leaving no large clumps.
- Place the plant in the hole and fill the hole with soil.
- Water thoroughly.
- Mulch with several inches of pine straw or fine pine bark.

Watering
- When the plant is young, water deeply every two weeks in spring, and every seven to ten days in summer.
- Once the shrub becomes established, water deeply during dry spells.

Easy Tip
Weigela is a good choice when you're looking for a shrub that will do well almost anywhere with little help.

Fertilizing
- Feed in early spring with a slow-release fertilizer for flowering shrubs.

Suggestions for Vigorous Growth
- Keep mulched year-round.
- After branches leaf out in spring, cut back tips that are dead from winter damage.
- If branches of 'Variegata' revert to plain green leaves, cut back to older wood.

Pest Control
- Few pests and diseases bother this plant.

Complementary Plants
- Plant in an evergreen shrub border where its flowers and foliage stand out.

Recommended Selections
- 'Bristol Ruby' has ruby-red flowers.
- 'Mont Blanc' is a large shrub with somewhat fragrant white blooms.
- 'Wine & Roses' has three-season appeal—new foliage is fresh green, flowers are pink-rose, and fall foliage is glossy burgundy-purple.

Useful Hint
The most ornamental weigela is the old-fashioned *Weigela florida* 'Variegata', whose leaves have a creamy-white margin; it has deep-rose flowers and grows to a tidy 4 to 6 feet.

Winterberry

Ilex verticillata

A Deciduous Holly with Glowing Sprays of Red Berries in Winter

Though winterberry isn't evergreen as are the Chinese and Japanese hollies, its multitudes of intense-red berries are eye catching in early winter after the autumn leaves have fallen. The warm-gray bark contrasts nicely with the berries. Birds love the berries so much that a week of warm weather early in December may lead to their mass intoxication. Make sure you have both a male and a female plant if you want prodigious berry production.

Top Reasons to Plant

- Showy red berries in fall
- Attracts birds
- Likes moist soil
- Easy to grow
- Few pests and diseases
- Excellent for winter garden

Useful Hint

If the birds leave you any berries as late as the holidays, winterberry makes wonderful indoor arrangements in a vase of water—it's also beautiful out in the snow with a cardinal munching away at the berries.

Bloom Color
Inconspicuous white blossoms, followed by gorgeous berries

Bloom Period
Spring, with berries in fall

Height/Width
6 to 10 feet x 6 to 8 feet

Planting Location
- Moist, even wet, acidic soil
- Sun or a little light afternoon shade

Planting
- Plant in fall or spring.
- Make sure each group of female cultivars has at least one male—such as 'Apollo', 'Raritan Chief', or 'Jim Dandy'—to pollinate it.
- Dig the hole three times as wide as and the same depth as the rootball.
- Thoroughly break up the soil.
- Place the plant in the hole, setting it at the same depth it was growing, and fill the hole with soil.
- Water thoroughly.
- Mulch with several inches of pine straw or fine pine bark.

Watering
- Watering is rarely needed except for a few times after the shrub has been planted.

Fertilizing
- Feed with 1 tablespoon of 10-10-10 fertilizer per foot of plant height in spring and again in midsummer.

Easy Tip
Winterberries are all very hardy, large shrubs excellent for a natural landscape.

Suggestions for Vigorous Growth
- No pruning is required, though it's fine to cut berry branches for indoor use.
- To rejuvenate overgrown plants, in early spring cut one-third of the stems back to ground level each year for three years.

Pest Control
- No serious insects or diseases trouble this plant.

Complementary Plants
- Put ferns and other moisture-loving but sun-averse plants in winterberry's shade.
- Plant against an evergreen backdrop for a beautiful effect—Prague viburnum, osmanthus, and Leyland cypress are good choices.

Recommended Selections
- *Ilex verticillata* 'Winter Red' is the most commonly available winterberry—it has dark-green leaves and profuse berries.
- 'Sparkleberry', a cross between *I. verticillata* and *I. decidua*, is perhaps the showiest of all the winterberries, bearing a heavy crop of large, scarlet fruits—it must be pollinated with 'Apollo'.

Winter Daphne

Daphne odora

A Demanding Diva That Pays Off with Divine Winter Fragrance

On a cold February or March day, when you're wondering if anything is still alive in your garden, a single bloom of daphne is enough to remind you that spring will come again. Even when very small, daphne cheers the soul with its delightful, pervasive fragrance. Though it needs very well-drained soil, just the right amount of sun, and careful removal of diseased leaves, daphne is well worth the effort.

Top Reasons to Plant

- Clusters of small rosy-pink flowers
- Delightful fragrance
- Blooms in late winter
- Thick, glossy evergreen leaves
- Good cut flower

Useful Hint

The key to success with winter daphne is careful attention to placing and preparing the soil.

Bloom Color
Rosy-pink

Bloom Period
Late winter

Height/Width
2 to 4 feet x 2 to 4 feet

Planting Location
- Very well-drained, fertile soil
- Sun but with midday shade

Planting
- Plant in early spring.
- Dig the hole twice as wide as and one and one-half times as deep as the rootball.
- Mix 1 part soil with 1 part coarse builder's or pea gravel and 2 parts fine pine bark.
- Place the plant in the hole so the top of the rootball is slightly higher than ground level.
- Fill the hole with soil.
- Water thoroughly.
- Mulch with several inches of pine straw or fine pine bark.

Watering
- Water enough to keep the plant from wilting.
- Overwatering causes root rot—a usually fatal problem that is daphne's biggest enemy.

Fertilizing
- Feed in spring and again in midsummer with 1 tablespoon of 10-10-10 fertilizer per foot of plant height.

Easy Tip

For a wonderful February treat, cut a few of the nosegay-type flowers and float them in a bowl with camellia blossoms.

Suggestions for Vigorous Growth
- This plant needs no pruning.
- Keep 2 inches of mulch over the roots year-round, but pull the mulch 3 inches away from the stem to prevent stem rot.

Pest Control
- Poor siting and care result in problems with root rot and leaf disease.

Complementary Plants
- Use in the perennial border for a beautiful effect.
- Plant near a door where the fragrance and flowers can be enjoyed.

Recommended Selections
- 'Aureomarginata' has a white margin around each leaf.
- *Daphne* x *burkwoodii* 'Carol Mackie' is less fragrant but also less demanding.

Witchhazel

Hamamelis × intermedia

A Wonderful Winter Spirit-Lifter

Few are the shrubs flowering in February, but witchhazel flowers in late winter and has a pleasant scent with intensely colored fall foliage as well. The narrow, twisting petals occur in clusters up and down the branches, virtually covering the upper two-thirds of the plant. Flower colors range from yellow to orange to red, and since they appear when the shrub is leafless, their effect is dramatic, even in the gloom of a February evening.

Top Reasons to Plant

- Winter blooms in bright colors
- Fragrant flowers
- Good fall color
- Easy to grow
- Pest and disease resistant
- Adaptable to varying soils

Useful Hint

The bark of the common witchhazel (*Hamamelis virginiana*) is the source of witchhazel liniment.

Bloom Color
Shades of yellow, red, and orange

Bloom Period
Winter

Height/Width
5 to 10 feet x 4 to 8 feet

Planting Location
• Moist, fertile soil with lots of organic matter—good in clay soil
• Sun to light shade

Planting
• Plant in fall.
• Read the plant's label to ensure proper spacing for its mature size.
• Dig the hole three times as wide as and slightly shallower than the rootball.
• Thoroughly break up the soil, leaving no large clods.
• Place the plant in the hole, untangling the roots if necessary, and spread them in the hole.
• Fill the hole with soil and water thoroughly.
• Mulch with several inches of pine straw.

Watering
• Water regularly to keep the soil evenly moist.
• In hot, dry weather, check twice weekly to make sure the soil isn't dry.

Easy Tip
Cut budded branches of witchhazel, take them indoors, and put them in a vase for winter blooms.

Fertilizing
• Feed with 1 tablespoon of 10-10-10 fertilizer per foot of plant height in March, June, and August.

Suggestions for Vigorous Growth
• Maintain 3 inches of mulch year-round.
• Prune to control size in late March.

Pest Control
• This plant has few or no pest problems.

Complementary Plants
• Place where it can be seen and admired from indoors in winter.
• Place in front of large evergreen shrubs such as Burford holly where the flowers will show off.

Recommended Selections
• 'Diane' is the best red-flowered variety.
• 'Primavera' has bright-yellow flowers.

Yaupon Holly
Ilex vomitoria

An Easy-Care Evergreen with Bright-Red Berries

It's a good thing most purchasers don't know the Latin name for this excellent native shrub, or they might worry about its making them sick. The name refers to a body-cleansing tonic made by Native Americans that only a committed anthropologist could enjoy. Yaupon holly is very hardy and has beautiful red berries not as attractive to birds as many holly berries, so they glisten like jewels under the green leaves and remain until spring.

Top Reasons to Plant

○ Evergreen foliage
○ Bright-scarlet berries all winter
○ Easy to grow
○ Few pests and diseases
○ Versatile uses

Useful Hint

Yaupon holly can achieve the same look as the Japanese hollies but with only half the attention to pruning and watering.

Bloom Color
White, followed by showy red berries

Bloom Period
Spring with berries in fall and winter

Height/Width
8 to 15 feet x 6 to 10 feet

Planting Location
• Any soil, wet or dry
• Sun to shade, but grows slowly in shade

Planting
• Plant in fall or spring.
• Dig the hole three times as wide as and the same depth as the rootball.
• Thoroughly break up the soil, leaving no large clumps.
• Place the plant in the hole, spreading out the roots and making sure the plant is at the same depth as it was growing.
• Pack the soil around the roots and water thoroughly.
• Mulch with 3 inches of pine straw.

Watering
• Water for a few weeks after planting.
• Once established, Yaupon holly tolerates dry soils.

Fertilizing
• During the first year, feed in March, June, and September with 1 tablespoon of 10-10-10 fertilizer per foot of plant height.
• After the first year, feed in April and June using the same amount of fertilizer.

Easy Tip
Yaupon holly is an excellent choice for either a wet or a dry problem site.

Suggestions for Vigorous Growth
• Prune in March to make the plant more dense.
• Severe pruning may be done in February, and regrowth will be rapid in spring—cut back new sprouts by half after they reach 12 inches long.

Pest Control
• No serious pests or diseases bother this shrub.

Complementary Plants
• Use as a foundation plant to replace languishing Japanese holly or Kurume azalea.
• Plant as a tall screen.
• Prune to form a short, rounded mass.

Recommended Selections
• 'Pendula', the weeping form, is a mainstay of commercial landscapers.
• 'Schillings' grows only 3 feet high and wide and is an excellent choice for a foundation shrub.

Gardening Basics

We often tell beginning gardeners that if they haven't moved a plant three times, it's probably not yet in the right place. We take comfort in what our friend, nurseryman Bud Heist, says: "Don't say we can't grow it, just say we don't yet know what it needs."

Before you consider the light, drainage, and exposure in your favorite garden spot, spend a little time learning about the soil, nutrients, pests, and plant diseases common in your area.

Soil

Some roots are reputed to be able to crack a house foundation or to break up a sidewalk, but roots are actually quite tender. When you put a plant in the soil, whether it is Bermuda grass or a baby oak, the roots will grow in the direction where resistance is least. Roots grow in the parts of the soil that offer moisture, oxygen, and nutrients.

Plants prefer to grow in soil that is a blend of clay, sand, and organic matter. The water and oxygen required by roots are plentiful in such an environment, and nutrients are available throughout. But few gardeners are blessed with perfect soil. The clay soil so abundant in north Georgia tends to have lots of moisture but little oxygen. The sandy soil prevalent along the coast has lots of oxygen but holds little water and few nutrients. The quickest way to make your soil better is to add more nutrients in the form of compost or other organic matter.

Organic Matter

Organic matter is found in manure, compost, and other materials. Ground pine bark is a common soil amendment found throughout the state of Georgia. Gardeners in the southern part of the state use ground peanut hulls. Peat moss is readily available, but it doesn't seem to persist in our soil as long as the coarser materials do. You may purchase your organic soil amendments, but if you learn how to produce them from good compost or if you find a good source of manure, you can have an unlimited free supply of organic matter.

Compost

Ever wonder why good gardeners wax eloquent about manure and compost? It's because either element, when added to a garden, can double the size and vigor of the plants. Some gardeners swear they achieve triple success when they add one of these materials to their ordinary soil. You might say that successful gardeners don't have green thumbs, they have black thumbs...from all of the manure and compost they've handled!

The reason compost is superior to any other source of organic matter is that it is *alive*. Compost is the decomposed remains of leaves, lawn clippings, pruned branches, and discarded stalks. The billions of fungi, bacteria, and other living creatures in compost are important parts of any healthy soil. Unfortunately, if you are gardening in a spot that is hard and bare, the soil has very little life in it. Plants growing in hard soil can be made beautiful, but they require more fertilizer and water to keep them looking their best.

Compost is the lazy gardener's friend. It contains billions of living creatures that help roots absorb water and nutrients. These tiny gardeners can take over some of the tasks of fertilizing and watering your plants.

Making compost never has to be complicated. Mother Nature has been composting for millions of years, and she never used a pitchfork or compost bin or expensive compost starter. Some gardeners choose to compost on a large scale, lugging bags of their neighbors' leaves up the street to dump on their compost piles. Others just throw their own leaves and clippings onto a pile and let nature take its course. Either method is fine. But the forming of compost does take time. It takes approximately six months and a thirty-gallon bag of yard trimmings to manufacture one cubic foot of compost. Mixing and turning a compost pile once a month can make the process go a bit faster.

While it's easy to make compost, it might be even easier to buy soil amendments at a garden center. But how much of this supplemental material does one need to make a difference in the soil? Dr. Tim Smalley, Professor of Horticulture at the University of Georgia, recommends spreading a layer of compost two inches thick over a garden flower bed and then mixing it with the soil underneath. In practical terms, that's two cubic feet of soil conditioner for every eight square feet of flower bed. You can see why composters are caught "borrowing" their neighbors' leaves at night!

The organic matter should be mixed to a depth of six to eight inches in the soil. With the addition of organic matter the soil will loosen, and it will stay loose for years. Oxygen will penetrate to where the roots are growing. The organic matter will absorb excess water and hold it in reserve for the plant to use when drier times come.

Watering

It seems simple enough to water an outdoor plant, but most gardeners either over-water or under-water their plants. Proper watering is accomplished differently in different parts of the state. Sandy soil drains so well that water must be applied twice a week during a blistering summer. Clay soil holds too much water. Plants in clay soil must be watered less often, or they will succumb to root rot.

The amount of water to use also differs among plants. A shallow-rooted fern might need one-fourth gallon of water applied every other day. A densely rooted lawn requires six hundred gallons per thousand square feet every week. A new tree might require three gallons twice a week for one month and afterwards only need watering when a drought occurs.

113

Your own observations are best when you are determining when and how much to water. Here are some tips to get you started:

- Water container plants until the water runs out the bottom.
- Do not water again until the top inch of soil is dry.
- Put a hose at the base of a newly installed plant and thoroughly soak the root ball once a week. As the plant begins to grow larger, take into consideration that the size of the root zone will also increase.
- Use shallow cans to measure the amount of water applied by your lawn sprinkler. Put six cans in the area being sprinkled and run the system for an hour. Then measure the depth of water in all of the cans. If the average depth of water is one-half inch, you will know the grass root zone has been irrigated. This may take one to two hours.
- If summer restrictions limit your watering, determine which plants would cost the most to replace, and water them first. It makes more sense to save a specimen maple tree than to keep ten dollars worth of petunias alive.
- An inexpensive water timer and a few soaker hoses can be a gardener's best friends.

Mulch

If a plant's roots are subjected to a long Georgia drought, even the toughest plant in the finest soil will suffer. Mulching will help you avoid this problem. Georgia's millions of pine trees give us two of the best mulches in the world, pine straw and pine bark chips. Mulch acts like a blanket. It keeps moisture in the soil, and it prevents plant roots from becoming too hot or too cold. Other good mulches include shredded fall leaves, wood chips, and shredded cypress bark. Few gardeners succeed without placing a one- to two-inch layer of mulch on top of the soil around all of their plants.

Nutrients

Plants need nitrogen, phosphorus, and potassium in order to grow well. When you buy a bag of fertilizer, you will see three numbers on the label. These numbers indicate the amounts of nitrogen, phosphorus, and potassium in the fertilizer. The numbers represent the percentage of each nutrient in the mixture. For example, a bag of 10-10-10 fertilizer contains 10% nitrogen (N), 10% phosphorus (P), and 10% potassium (K). The other 70% is just clay.

Each nutrient serves a function in the overall good health of a plant. So how do you know which fertilizer to buy when your garden center offers dozens of combinations of the three nutrient numbers? Just look at the numbers on the bag and remember: Up, Down, and All Around.

Up: Nitrogen promotes leaf growth. That's why lawn fertilizer has a high nitrogen percentage. A common turf fertilizer is a 16-4-8, but some brands have even more nitrogen than this. Grass leaves are mowed off constantly, so nitrogen is needed to help grow more of them.

Down: Phosphorus is important in the formation of roots and is very important for flower, seed, and fruit growth. That's why so-called "starter fertilizers" and "bloom fertilizers" have high percentages of phosphorus.

All Around: Potassium increases overall cell health. When your plant is under stress from drought or from cold, adequate potassium helps the plant withstand the crisis. "Winterizer" fertilizer for lawns is a good choice for grass that must endure such conditions. Its potassium percentage is high to help the grass fight winter cold damage.

It is not necessary to buy a different fertilizer for each of the plant types you have in your landscape. You really can't hurt a plant by applying the wrong fertilizer. Your perennials won't be damaged by the application of "azalea fertilizer." The lawn won't be hurt if you fertilize it with 10-10-10. There may be some situations in which one type of fertilizer is marginally better; for example, a "slow-release turf fertilizer" might be especially desirable for some types of grass. But you can do quite well with the purchase of just three main types of fertilizer: 16-4-8 for your lawn, 6-12-12 for new plants, and 10-10-10 for everything else.

How do you know what amount of fertilizer to apply? How much nutrition does your soil already hold? Do you need any lime? To find out, you need to perform a soil test.

Soil Test

There are two ways to test your soil. You can purchase an inexpensive gardener's test kit with simple chemicals and test tubes and do it yourself, or you can take some of your soil to your local county Extension Service office for a low-cost analysis.

Test kits are economical and simple to use. To use one, you'll mix your soil with water, then add a few drops of indicator chemical that will cause the water to change color. If you feel confident that you can match the color of the water with the colors on the small color wheel that is provided, you can determine which nutrients you need to add to your soil. If you don't trust your powers of analysis, you might want to compare your conclusions with those of the University of Georgia Soil Testing Laboratory through your local county Extension Service office.

Having soil tested by the Extension Service is a simple process as well. Collect several scoops of dirt from different areas of your yard and mix them together. The Extension Service needs just one cup of this soil mixture for the test. Put the soil in a bag, take it to your local Extension office, and tell the Extension agent what you intend to grow in it. The soil will be shipped to a laboratory in Athens. Within ten days you will receive a mailed report describing the nutrients present in your soil, the amounts in which they are present, and specific recommendations for correct fertilizer use.

Lime

Though lime does not offer plant nutrients (aside from calcium, which plants need in small amounts), it helps plants absorb nutrients more efficiently. Georgia soils, particularly in the northern half of the state, tend to be acidic. In an acidic soil, plant roots can't collect the nitrogen, phosphorus, and potassium they need to function. Lime makes soil less acidic. Soil acidity is measured in numbers from 1 to 14 on what is called the pH scale. Most plants prefer soil that has a pH of 6.0 to 6.5. A hard clay subsoil may have a pH of 4.5. It takes a lot of lime to move the pH up to 6.5. Your soil test will determine the pH of your soil and the amount of lime it needs.

Pests and Diseases

The same conditions that make our gardens so beautiful make Georgia a happy homeland for insect and disease pests. A long growing season means that insect populations have time to explode each year. Our high humidity and warm temperatures are perfect for the growth of fungi and bacteria.

It cannot be said often enough that a healthy plant is the best defense against pests. A plant that grows vigorously can quickly overcome insect damage. A plant that is not stressed by its environment can resist disease spores. Many of the plants included in this book were chosen because of their strong resistance to insects and diseases. If you follow our recommendations about the proper placement of your plants and how to care for them, your garden will rarely need pesticides. If you choose the plant varieties we recommend, you will have genetic allies in your fight against pests.

Organic vs. Inorganic Gardening

If you find pests attacking your plants, what should you do? Is the problem bad enough to use a pesticide? Which pesticide should you use? Should you rely on synthetic chemicals or should you choose pesticides made from organic sources? These questions trouble all of us. Some gardeners prefer to use only organic pesticides. Others are more pragmatic, sometimes using synthetic pesticides, occasionally preferring organic ones, but always striving to use the smallest amounts possible in every case.

There is no single correct answer to the question: Which is best— organic or inorganic gardening? Synthetic pesticides for home gardeners have been repeatedly tested for safety by their manufacturers and by the federal government. Scientists and bureaucrats who advise us on environmental matters have declared that prudent use of approved pesticides offers fewer health risks than we would encounter if we avoided pesticides completely and endangered our food supply. Organic gardening does not always completely eliminate pesticide use, as it sometimes calls for the use of pesticides that come from organic sources. These organic pesticides may have risks higher or lower than synthetic ones. Fortunately, new gardening products with fewer risks appear on the market every year.

The choice between an "organic" or an "inorganic" garden is yours alone to make. You must decide whether the convenience of using synthetic pesticides offsets the hard work and constant vigilance required to completely eliminate their use.

Information on Pesticide Use

If you need advice on which pesticides to use, the best resource for assistance is the local office of the University of Georgia Cooperative Extension Service. The agents there maintain the latest research data on the most effective and least potentially harmful pesticides to use. Ask them to tell you about all of the alternatives for solving your pest problem. Then you can use your experience and wisdom to make the choices that are best for your situation.

The Name Game

Gardeners may wonder why they need to know the scientific names of plants. The answer is simple: you want to make sure the rose you purchase for your own garden is the same sweet-smelling rose you admired (and coveted) in your neighbor's garden. It's true that scientific names, which are derived from Latin or Greek, can be long and hard to pronounce. But unlike a common plant name, which often is applied to two very different plants, a scientific designation is specific and unique.

Throughout this book we identify plants by both their scientific and common names. A plant's scientific name consists of the genus (the first word) and an epithet. For example, all maples belong to the genus Acer. The epithet (in our example, rubrum) identifies a specific kind of maple. *Acer rubrum* is a red maple. The genus and epithet are always italicized and the genus name begins with a capital letter, while the entire epithet is always written in lower case.

A third word in the name may refer to a special variety of the plant, called a cultivar. The cultivar name is important because it designates a superior selection known for bigger blooms, better foliage, or some other noteworthy characteristic. A cultivar name is distinguished by the use of single quotation marks, as in the name Acer rubrum 'October Glory', a red maple with excellent fall leaf color. Most cultivars must be propagated by division or cuttings because they may not come true from seed.

A scientific name can change, but this happens only rarely, and there are certain rigid rules that apply to the practice of plant nomenclature. It is much easier to track down a wonderful plant if you know the full scientific name. Armed with a knowledge of both scientific and common names, you should be able to acquire the best plants for your Georgia garden.

Propagation

Once you become excited about gardening, you may develop "plant lust." You'll start to think that you must buy every new and exciting plant you discover. A much less expensive way to acquire your plants is to propagate them using seeds, cuttings, or divisions.

Growing annuals from seed works well, but it is usually the slowest method for propagating perennials and is not always successful. The good news is that once they are well established in your garden, many perennial plants can be easily divided and transplanted, providing a constant supply of new plants.

When dividing a perennial, dig up the entire plant and separate it into pieces. You may dig up a mature clump and use a digging fork and your fingers to tease apart the roots, or you can make a clean cut with a straight-edged shovel to divide the large clump into smaller pieces. Make sure each piece has roots and buds. Remember, always have the new garden area prepared ahead of time for the new divisions, and don't let the roots dry out. Once all the divisions are planted, water them well. They'll grow large in no time!

Rooting stem cuttings is another option for propagating both perennials and annuals, as well as many shrubs. The important point to remember about cuttings is to take cuttings during the correct season. Timing is more important with shrubs than with perennials and annuals. Rooting stem cuttings provides a simple means to overwinter a piece of an annual that has grown too big to save in its present size; thus, it can be preserved and propagated again.

Another easy method for propagating plants, including most azaleas and hydrangeas, is layering. Penny McHenry, president of the American Hydrangea Society and a keen Atlanta gardener, propagates some of her favorite hydrangeas by bending young branches so they touch the ground. Making sure to loosen the dirt at the point of contact, she places soil and organic matter on top of the stem and uses a brick to weigh it down. Within two months, Penny has a newly rooted plant that can be cut off from the main plant and transplanted to a new location.

These are just a few suggestions for ways to get more out of your garden or to share your bounty with friends. Some of the most wonderful gardens started with "a piece of this and a division of that." Who knows, you may develop your own favorite technique for propagating a special rose or that mildew-resistant phlox you discover in your garden!

With these few tips you now have an overview of the basic information needed to become a gardener. To obtain the truly valuable skills of gardening, you will have to practice the 4-H Club motto: Learn by Doing. You will have to don your old jeans, take up your shovel, and dig!

If you keep your heart and mind open to the nuances of nature, you will cultivate more than just pretty flowers and strong trees. Both your plants and you yourself will grow in your beautiful garden. Fayetteville nurseryman Steven Stinchcomb may have said it best: "Some people are just gardeners in their heads and some people become gardeners in their hearts."

Good Gardening!

Glossary

Alkaline soil: soil with a pH greater than 7.0. It lacks acidity, often because it has limestone in it.

All-purpose fertilizer: powdered, liquid, or granular fertilizer with a balanced proportion of the three key nutrients—nitrogen (N), phosphorus (P), and potassium (K). It is suitable for maintenance nutrition for most plants.

Annual: a plant that lives its entire life in one season. It is genetically determined to germinate, grow, flower, set seed, and die the same year.

Balled and burlapped: describes a tree or shrub grown in the field whose soilball was wrapped with protective burlap and twine when the plant was dug up to be sold or transplanted.

Bare root: describes plants that have been packaged without any soil around their roots. (Often young shrubs and trees purchased through the mail arrive with their exposed roots covered with moist peat or sphagnum moss, sawdust, or similar material, and wrapped in plastic.)

Barrier plant: a plant that has intimidating thorns or spines and is sited purposely to block foot traffic or other access to the home or yard.

Beneficial insects: insects or their larvae that prey on pest organisms and their eggs. They may be flying insects, such as ladybugs, parasitic wasps, praying mantids, and soldier bugs, or soil dwellers such as predatory nematodes, spiders, and ants.

Berm: a narrow, raised ring of soil around a tree, used to hold water so it will be directed to the root zone.

Bract: a modified leaf structure on a plant stem near its flower, resembling a petal. Often it is more colorful and visible than the actual flower, as in dogwood.

Bud union: the place where the top of a plant was grafted to the rootstock; usually refers to roses.

Canopy: the overhead branching area of a tree, usually referring to its extent including foliage.

Cold hardiness: the ability of a perennial plant to survive the winter cold in a particular area.

Composite: a flower that is actually composed of many tiny flowers. Typically, they are flat clusters of tiny, tight florets, sometimes surrounded by wider-petaled florets. Composite flowers are highly attractive to bees and beneficial insects.

Compost: organic matter that has undergone progressive decomposition by microbial and macrobial activity until it is reduced to a spongy, fluffy texture. Added to soil of any type, it improves the soil's ability to hold air and water and to drain well.

Corm: the swollen energy-storing structure, analogous to a bulb, under the soil at the base of the stem of plants such as crocus and gladiolus.

Crown: the base of a plant at, or just beneath, the surface of the soil where the roots meet the stems.

Cultivar: a CULTIvated VARiety. It is a naturally occurring form of a plant that has been identified as special or superior and is purposely selected for propagation and production.

Deadhead: a pruning technique that removes faded flower heads from plants to improve their appearances, abort seed production, and stimulate further flowering.

Deciduous plants: unlike evergreens, these trees and shrubs lose their leaves in the fall.

Desiccation: drying out of foliage tissues, usually due to drought or wind.

Division: the practice of splitting apart perennial plants to create several smaller-rooted segments. The practice is useful for controlling the plant's size and for acquiring more plants; it is also essential to the health and continued flowering of certain ones.

Dormancy: the period, usually the winter, when perennial plants temporarily cease active growth and rest. Dormant is the verb form, as used in this sentence: *Some plants, like spring-blooming bulbs, go dormant in the summer.*

Established: the point at which a newly planted tree, shrub, or flower begins to produce new growth, either foliage or stems. This is an indication that the roots have recovered from transplant shock and have begun to grow and spread.

Evergreen: perennial plants that do not lose their foliage annually with the onset of winter. Needled or broadleaf foliage will persist and continues to function on a plant through one or more winters, aging and dropping unobtrusively in cycles of three or four years or more.

Floret: a tiny flower, usually one of many forming a cluster, that comprises a single blossom.

Foliar: of or about foliage—usually refers to the practice of spraying foliage, as in fertilizing or treating with insecticide; leaf tissues absorb liquid directly for fast results, and the soil is not affected.

Germinate: to sprout. Germination is a fertile seed's first stage of development.

Graft (union): the point on the stem of a woody plant with sturdier roots where a stem from a highly ornamental plant is inserted so that it will join with it. Roses are commonly grafted.

Hardscape: the permanent, structural, nonplant part of a landscape, such as walls, sheds, pools, patios, arbors, and walkways.

Herbaceous: plants having fleshy or soft stems that die back with frost; the opposite of woody.

Hybrid: a plant that is the result of intentional or natural cross-pollination between two or more plants of the same species or genus.

Low water demand: describes plants that tolerate dry soil for varying periods of time. Typically, they have succulent, hairy, or silvery-gray foliage and tuberous roots or taproots.

Mulch: a layer of material over bare soil to protect it from erosion and compaction by rain, and to discourage weeds. It may be inorganic (gravel, fabric) or organic (wood chips, bark, pine needles, chopped leaves).

Naturalize: (*a*) to plant seeds, bulbs, or plants in a random, informal pattern as they would appear in their natural habitats; (*b*) to adapt to and spread throughout adopted habitats (a tendency of some nonnative plants).

Nectar: the sweet fluid produced by glands on flowers that attract pollinators such as hummingbirds and honeybees, for whom it is a source of energy.

Organic material, organic matter: any material or debris that is derived from plants. It is carbon-based material capable of undergoing decomposition and decay.

Peat moss: organic matter from peat sedges (United States) or sphagnum mosses (Canada), often used to improve soil texture. The acidity of sphagnum peat moss makes it ideal for boosting or maintaining soil acidity while also improving its drainage.

Perennial: a flowering plant that lives over two or more seasons. Many die back with frost, but their roots survive the winter and generate new shoots in the spring.

pH: a measurement of the relative acidity (low pH) or alkalinity (high pH) of soil or water based on a scale of 1 to 14, 7 being neutral. Individual plants require soil to be within a certain range so that nutrients can dissolve in moisture and be available to them.

Pinch: to remove tender stems and/or leaves by pressing them between thumb and forefinger. This pruning technique encourages branching, compactness, and flowering in plants, or it removes aphids clustered at growing tips.

Pollen: the yellow, powdery grains in the center of a flower. A plant's male sex cells, they are transferred to the female plant parts by means of wind or animal pollinators to fertilize them and create seeds.

Raceme: an arrangement of single-stalked flowers along an elongated, unbranched axis.

Rhizome: a swollen energy-storing stem structure, similar to a bulb, that lies horizontally in the soil, with roots emerging from its lower surface and growth shoots from a growing point at or near its tip, as in bearded iris.

Rootbound (or potbound): the condition of a plant that has been confined in a container too long, its roots having been forced to wrap around themselves and even swell out of the container. Successful transplanting or repotting requires untangling and trimming away of some of the matted roots.

Root flare: the transition at the base of a tree trunk where the bark tissue begins to differentiate and roots begin to form just before entering the soil. This area should not be covered with soil when planting a tree.

Self-seeding: the tendency of some plants to sow their seeds freely around the yard. It creates many seedlings the following season that may or may not be welcome.

Semievergreen: tending to be evergreen in a mild climate but deciduous in a rigorous one.

Shearing: the pruning technique whereby plant stems and branches are cut uniformly with long-bladed pruning shears (hedge shears) or powered hedge trimmers. It is used when creating and maintaining hedges and topiary.

Slow-acting fertilizer: fertilizer that is water insoluble and therefore releases its nutrients gradually as a function of soil temperature, moisture, and related microbial activity. Typically granular, it may be organic or synthetic.

Succulent growth: the sometimes undesirable production of fleshy, water-storing leaves or stems that results from overfertilization.

Sucker: a new-growing shoot. Underground plant roots produce suckers to form new stems and spread by means of these suckering roots to form large plantings, or colonies. Some plants produce root suckers or branch suckers as a result of pruning or wounding.

Tuber: a type of underground storage structure in a plant stem, analogous to a bulb. It generates roots below and stems above ground (example: dahlia).

Variegated: having various colors or color patterns. The term usually refers to plant foliage that is streaked, edged, blotched, or mottled with a contrasting color—often green with yellow, cream, or white.

White grubs: fat, off-white, wormlike larvae of Japanese beetles. They reside in the soil and feed on plant (especially grass) roots until summer when they emerge as beetles to feed on plant foliage.

Wings: (a) the corky tissue that forms edges along the twigs of some woody plants such as winged euonymus; (b) the flat, dried extension of tissue on some seeds, such as maple, that catch the wind and help them disseminate.

Bibliography

Armitage, Allan. 1989. *Herbaceous Perennial Plants: A Treatise on Their Culture and Garden Attributes*. Varsity Press, Inc. Athens, GA.

Bender, Steven and Felder Rushing. 1993. *Passalong Plants*. The University of North Carolina Press. Chapel Hill, NC.

Brooklyn Botanic Garden. *Plants and Gardens Handbooks*, many different subjects. List available from Brooklyn Botanic Garden, 1000 Washington Ave., Brooklyn, NY.

Burke, Ken (ed.). 1980. *Shrubs and Hedges*. The American Horticultural Society. Franklin Center, PA.

Burke, Ken (ed.). 1982. *Gardening in the Shade*. The American Horticultural Society, Franklin Center, PA.

Dirr, Michael. 1990. *Manual of Woody Landscape Plants*. Stipes Publishing. Champaign, IL.

Gardiner, J.M. 1989. *Magnolias*. Globe Pequot Press, Chester, PA.

Gates, Galen et al. 1994. *Shrubs and Vines*. Pantheon Books. New York, NY.

Greenlee, John. 1992. *The Encyclopedia of Ornamental Grasses*. Rodale Press. Emmaus, PA.

Halfacre, R. Gordon and Anne R. Shawcroft. 1979. *Landscape Plants of the Southeast*. Sparks Press. Raleigh, NC.

Harper, Pamela and Frederick McGourty. 1985. *Perennials: How to Select, Grow and Enjoy*. HP Books. Tucson, AZ.

Heath, Brent and Becky. 1995. *Daffodils for American Gardens*. Elliott & Clark Publishing. Washington, DC.

Hipps, Carol Bishop. 1994. *In a Southern Garden*. Macmillan Publishing. New York, NY.

Lawrence, Elizabeth. 1991. *A Southern Garden*. The University of North Carolina Press. Chapel Hill, NC.

Lawson-Hall, Toni and Brian Rothera. 1996. *Hydrangeas*. Timber Press. Portland, OR.

Loewer, Peter. 1992. *Tough Plants for Tough Places*. Rodale Press. Emmaus, PA.

Mikel, John. 1994. *Ferns for American Gardens*. Macmillan Publishing. New York, NY.

Ogden, Scott. 1994. *Garden Bulbs for the South*. Taylor Publishing. Dallas, TX.

Still, Steven. 1994. *Manual of Herbaceous Ornamental Plants*. 4th edition. Stipes Publishing. Champaign, IL.

Vengris, Jonas and William A. Torello. 1982. *Lawns*. Thomson Publications. Fresno, CA.

Winterrowd, Wayne. 1992. *Annuals for Connoisseurs*. Prentice Hall. New York, NY.

Photography Credits

Thomas Eltzroth: pages 11, 16, 22, 30, 32, 36, 38, 46, 58, 60, 64, 66, 70, 74, 76, 90, 92, 96, 98

Jerry Pavia: pages 9, 10, 18, 28, 34, 42, 44, 48, 56, 72, 82, 84, 86, 104, 108

Liz Ball and Rick Ray: pages 12, 14, 26, 54, 62, 68, 88, 94, 102, 106

Pam Harper: pages 40, 78, 80, 100

Felder Rushing: pages 8, 20

William Adams: page 110

Lorenzo Gunn: page 52

Ralph Snodsmith: page 50

Andre Viette: page 24

Plant Index

Want to know more about Georgia gardening?

Interested in terrific trees for Georgia? Do you want healthful and tasty herbs, fruits, and vegetables from your Georgia garden? How about fantastic Georgia flowers?

If you enjoy *50 Great Shrubs for Georgia*, you will appreciate similar books featuring Georgia trees, vegetables (including fruits and herbs), and flowers. These valuable books also deserve a place in your gardening library.

50 Great Trees for Georgia

Erica Glasener and Walter Reeves recommend fifty great trees for Georgia. They offer fantastic options on small flowering trees, great evergreens, and trees that delight with multiseason interest.

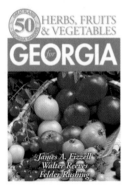

50 Great Herbs, Fruits and Vegetables for Georgia

If you are inclined to "edibles" in your Georgia garden, this is the book for you. It provides valuable advice on how to select, plant and grow tasty herbs, luscious fruits, and flavorful vegetables. Written by James A. Fizzell, Walter Reeves, and Felder Rushing, this book offers more than seventy-five years of gardening wisdom all in an easy to-use-format.

50 Great Flowers for Georgia

Erica Glasener and Walter Reeves share their personal recommendations on fifty delightful flowering plants for Georgia. From colorful annuals that give you spring-to-fall color, to hard-working perennials that return year after year, you will find much to choose from in this book.

Look for each of these books today.